Manchester Moorland Hikes

Nick Burton

Published by Sigma Leisure – an imprint of
Sigma Press, 1 South Oak Lane, Wilmslow, Cheshire SK9 6AR, England.

British Library Cataloguing in Publication Data
A CIP record for this book is available from the British Library.

ISBN: 1-85058-709-4

Typesetting and Design by: Sigma Press, Wilmslow, Cheshire.

Cover photograph: The Peel Tower above Holcombe village

Maps and photographs: Nick Burton

Printed by: MFP Design and Print

Disclaimer: the information in this book is given in good faith and is believed to be correct at the time of publication. No responsibility is accepted by either the author or publisher for errors or omissions, or for any loss or injury howsoever caused. Only you can judge your own fitness, competence and experience.

Preface

As a small boy growing up in the urban jungle of North Manchester, the nearest I got to a moor was Kersal Moor and the only hill I ever climbed was Cheetham Hill. It was only when I went to school in Astley Bridge, Bolton that I could look down on Manchester from a lofty height on the edge of the moors and view it in its natural setting. There they were, an intriguing line of distant hills rising above the Manchester metropolis, so near to the city and yet a world apart – the Pennines had caught me in its spell!

This book intends to reunite Manchester with its moors, enabling urban dwellers to experience dramatic and often challenging walks without having to travel great distances from home. There is nothing quite so uplifting as looking down on the hustle and bustle of urban life from the splendid solitude of a moorland peak. Spend half a day or a whole day exploring the moors and monuments on the edge of the city and, preferably, go when visibility conditions are good – for all the walks have spectacular long-distance views of the Manchester region and beyond when the weather is behaving itself. In all the walks, you can look one way to pick out the city centre office blocks, the Town Hall and Salford Quays, then look another way to view such sights as Kinder Scout, Ingleborough and Penyghent, the Lancashire coast and even the Welsh Mountains.

In writing this book I would like to acknowledge the professional expertise and support provided by Graham Beech and staff at Sigma Press. One author, Gladys Sellers, should also be mentioned as her books are an excellent source of reference – in particular, "Walks on the West Pennine Moors"(1979) and "Walking in the South Pennines"(1991) both published by Cicerone Press.

Now put on those walking boots, pick up your anorak and mintcake and go hiking!

Nick Burton.

I dedicate this book to my wife Louise.

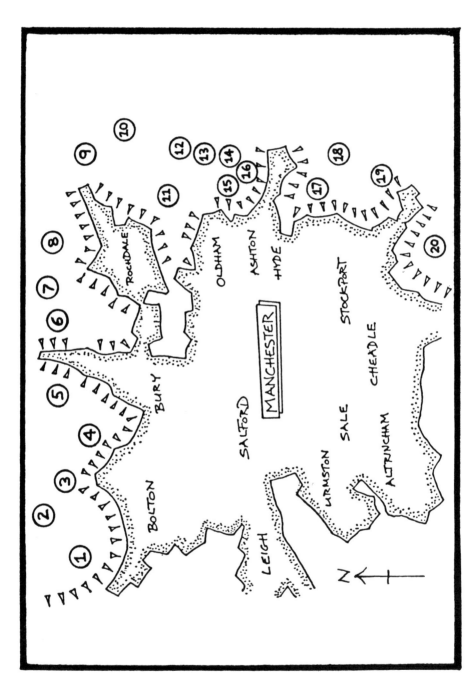

Contents

Introduction

The Walks

The 20 circular walks in this book are arranged geographically and are intended to cover all the uplands on the fringes of the vast urban region we now call 'Greater' Manchester. Starting north of the city the walks run west to east along the western spur of the Pennines which stretches above Bolton, Bury and Rochdale and separates Greater Manchester from Rossendale. The walks then run north to south along the edge of the main Pennine chain of hills, covering the high moors that overlook Rochdale, Oldham, Ashton, Stalybridge and also the Peak District foothills that reach out to the suburbs of Stockport and Marple.

It is hoped that the walks will act as a guide to all those hills and moorland monuments seen from the towns below, but which are often overlooked. I aim to make these hills more identifiable to the rambler by exploring and describing them in detail. The walks vary in length from 4 miles to 14 ½ miles and explore a variety of moorlands, from gentle ridges such as Werneth Low and Mellor Moor to such bleak and boggy Pennine giants as Hoarstone Edge and White Hill. Many of the walks also share the same starting point or have sections of linking paths, thus allowing walks to be combined to create more challenging routes within the 20 miles plus bracket.

The walks do not cover every single moor and hill summit on the fringes of the city, as this would require a book twice this size and, in fact, many of the moors omitted are too uninteresting to visit or are not accessible by rights of way. However, all the distinctive hills and moorland groups are included and after completing the 20 walks in this book the hiker will have a comprehensive knowledge and understanding of the geography of the Manchester region. If you work in a high-rise city centre office with long-distance views to the Pennines, I guarantee you will be able to impress your work colleagues by naming all the distinctive ridges to be seen. No longer will they call you the office bore!

Each expedition, be it short or long, has been chosen to provide excellent views across the Manchester region and I would, therefore, suggest that to get the most out of these walks they be undertaken in clear conditions. Not always possible I know but it is worth waiting for the right day to appreciate the long-distance panoramas on offer. A note on what you are likely to see is outlined below but it is also worth noting that hot sunny days in the middle of summer do not guarantee good visibility over long distances. Even in short periods of dry sunny weather the views may be limited by a heat haze and atmospheric dust. The best visibility comes usually after rain showers have washed all the air pollution away, especially the city smog, and then the sun comes out. Sunny winter days can be just as ideal to get those views to the Welsh Mountains or to Pendle Hill and the Yorkshire Dales.

The Views

In ideal conditions, the following is a brief summary of what can commonly be seen on these hikes:

All the walks at some point give a view of the city, obviously from a variety of angles. The large cluster of city centre tower blocks makes central Manchester easy to recognise and, a few miles away, a smaller collection of shimmering glass structures can be recognised as Salford Quays. To the east of the city, the three large Audenshaw reservoirs surrounded by urban sprawl are easy to spot and can be clearly seen from all the walks on the main Pennine chain.

Other towns that are distinctive are Rochdale and Oldham. Rochdale has seven tower blocks (by Hopwood Hall College) in its centre and Oldham has one high rise block perched on a hill. Bolton is harder to spot, but the Gothic structure of its Town Hall can often be made out from the walks on the West Pennine Moors. In East Manchester, Ashton, Stalybridge and Hyde are lost in a mass sprawl, but the council towers of Hattersley usually stand out – unfortunately.

Of the hills themselves, there are many distinctive monuments and masts to be found and these are described in each of the walks. On a clear day anywhere on the Pennine fringes, you should be able to pick out in particular:

* Winter Hill with its huge TV masts
* The Peel Tower on Holcombe Moor
* Steep-sided Knowl Hill above Heywood
* The black crags of Blackstone Edge, and the Windy Hill radio mast
* The 'Pots and Pans' obelisk above Saddleworth
* The towers and monuments on Hartshead Pike, Werneth Low and Bishop Park, Oldham.

Looking further afield, the Manchester urban scene gives way to the flat Cheshire plain further south and Ringway's air terminal, Jodrell Bank and, possibly, the low ridge of hills above Helsby and Frodsham come into view. Looking south-west the huge cooling towers of Fiddler's Ferry Power Station along the Mersey Valley are a dominating feature and behind them on the clearest of days rise the faint outline of the Clwydian Hills and, possibly, even Snowdonia's mountains.

Looking east, the Kinder Plateau, Longdendale and the huge Holme Moss transmitter are familiar sites as the Pennines roll away towards Derbyshire and Yorkshire. Looking north, the walks on the Rossendale Hills offer views of the Calder Valley, the Cliviger Moors, Pendle Hill, the Forest of Bowland and the peaks of Ingleborough and Penyghent in the Yorkshire Dales. The western edge of the West Pennine Moors, namely Rivington Pike, gives an exclusive view to the Lancashire coast – easily recognised by Blackpool Tower – and, on exceptional days, to the Lake District .

If you don't see all this the first time, do the walk again another day!

Geography and Geology of the Manchester region

In simple terms, the city centre lies at the heart of an embayment or basin, a low-lying area at the confluence of the Rivers Irk, Irwell and Medlock, the latter two of which rise in the uplands that encircle the basin to the north and east. The natural basin, covered in glacial till deposited by retreating ice sheets thousands of years ago, has proved ideal for the development of the metropolis. The industrial towns surrounding the city to the north and east are all situated on naturally advantageous sites associated with higher ground or rivers.

Surrounding the Manchester basin are two main areas of rock uplift – the Pennine Anticline, running north-south to the east of the city and the Rossendale Dome, running east-west to the north of the city and appearing as a high spur stretching out from the main Pennine axis. The western end of the Rossendale Dome – from the Irwell Valley to Rivington- is commonly referred to as the West Pennine Moors. It is all a lot more complex than this, as both the Pennine and Rossendale uplifts have been affected by geological faults – which include the Irwell Valley – as well as glaciation and river systems. Both uplifts created hills that were much higher than they are today but, after several thousand years of denudation, the hill ridges are now made up of horizontal layers of sedimentary rocks (of the Upper Carboniferous Period) characterised by sandstones known as the Millstone Grits and Coal Measures, both including bands of weaker shales.

Industrial towns such as Bolton, Bury and Oldham to the north of the city are based on the coal-bearing Coal Measures, whilst the moors above them are dominated by the Millstone Grits with alternating bands of sandstone and less resistant shale. The steep-sided, flat-topped appearance of many moors and hills is due to the erosion and weathering of the shale bands at a greater rate than the more resistant sandstone above.

One other thing to note, the western flanks of the Pennines are all scarp slopes with steep-sided western edges and more gently rolling eastern slopes. To examine this, stand on the summit of Hollingworthall Moor (Walk 16) and note the steep scarp slopes to the north and south which overlook the industrial towns. This geographical feature is a result of the angle of dip of the rock beds, which dips more steeply to the west than east.

Moorland Access and Safety

The basic principle of walking the moors is: be prepared! Weather conditions can change in an instant and you should always make sure you have a windproof and waterproof jacket with you particularly if the weather looks unsettled. Take provisions with you and always take the relevant map (listed under each of the walks) as my sketch maps are not intended to take the place of the excellent and essential Ordnance Survey 1:25 000 scale maps. In poor conditions, I have recommended that a compass be taken on some of the more bleak walks but I also suggest that if the weather looks that bad, save the walk for a better day so that you can enjoy the views. Finally, if you can, let someone know where you are going just in case you are stuck out on the moors. Some of the walks (particularly Walks 10 and 12) are strenuous so, if you are a beginner, save them until last. They are both worthy conclusions to this collection of walks.

I have attempted to stick to rights of way, permissive paths and Access Areas as much as possible, though this is sometimes to the detriment of the walks since some hill summits are missed. There is no accepted 'freedom to roam' law in this country as yet and I am not going to encourage anyone to climb over fences, walls and gates particularly when stock are at large. However, some of the paths used are not definitive rights of way but are well-used by the public and many of these are often waymarked with stiles provided. I have presumed such routes to be accepted as permissive rights of way and hope that they will not be taken away from recreational use in the near future. As far as I am concerned, if a hiker is going quietly along his or her way and is aware of the country code, they will be doing no harm to anyone or anything.

1. Winter Hill

This walk goes through the picturesque hamlet of Barrow Bridge and climbs through pastures to a high moorland ridge and an old road leading to the spectacular viewpoint of Rivington Pike. It then crosses open moorland to the summit masts of Winter Hill before descending the moor along a celebrated right of way to the historic Smithills Hall. Note that a map and compass may be necessary in misty conditions to cross the moor from Rivington Pike to Winter Hill.

Peaks and Panoramas: RIVINGTON PIKE is a distinctive mound on which sits a restored 18th century square tower. The Pike offers the most extensive views throughout the West Pennines and on the clearest of days a panorama can be seen stretching from the Welsh Hills to the Lake District and including the West Lancashire Plain, the Fylde Coast and Morecambe Bay. Blackpool Tower is often visible along with Chorley, Preston and Southport. Much closer at hand are the Reebok Stadium, Horwich and Bolton. WINTER HILL is the highest point on the West Pennine Moors and is easily identifiable by its massive TV mast and transmitter station. Also littering its summit are a triangulation pillar, a plethora of radio masts, the monument known as Scotsman's Stump and a road! The best views from Winter Hill are revealed from its lower slopes leading to Smithills Dean when the vista opens up to Bolton, Greater Manchester and the Pennines.

Distance: 9½ miles

Map: Ordnance Survey Explorer Sheet No. 19 West Pennine Moors

Start: Smithills Country Park, Smithills Hall car park, Smithills Dean Road, Bolton (Grid Reference 699 119).

Getting there: Smithills Hall is situated 2 miles north of Bolton town centre and is just off the A58 ring road, Moss Bank Way. Smithills Dean Road is on the north side of the busy junction between Moss Bank Way and Halliwell Road. The entrance to the Hall is signposted and is on the right-hand side of the road just after passing Smithills School. Park on the Hall car park though there is a separate car park for the Smithills Coaching House inn and restaurant.

Public transport: A bus service from Bolton to Smithills stops directly outside the driveway entrance to Smithills Hall on Smithills Dean Road.

Background

A large chunk of Bolton's history lies in the first couple of miles of this walk, which take you from the medieval manor house of Smithills Hall to the industrial hamlet of Barrow Bridge. Much of Smithills Hall dates from the 15th century with later additions and it is now a museum at the centre of a country park. The Coach House and Stables nearby are also listed buildings. On the way into Barrow Bridge is a prominent roadside chimney, restored by Fred Dibnah, Bolton's celebrity steeplejack, in 1996. The chimney is all that remains of the 19th century spinning mills that stood along the brook and led to the formation of a 'model' village at Barrow Bridge. Rows of workers' cottages were built along Bazley Street which takes its name from Thomas Bazley, the entrepreneur who founded the community in 1846. Further up the main road through the village are more extravagant dwellings alongside the brook which were once occupied by mill management. The steep 63 steps, which lead uphill at the northern end of Barrow Bridge, were used by workers going to work on moorland collieries, including Burnt Edge colliery.

In the 19th century, many of these workers may have headed for Rivington Pike for the annual Whit Sunday Fair. The Pike was on private land until the estate was bought by soap magnate, William Hesketh Lever, later Lord Leverhulme, who bequeathed it to Bolton Corporation in 1900 for use as a park. The Pike was certainly used as a medieval beacon site and was lit in 1588 to warn of the approach of the Spanish Armada. They had not sailed up the River Douglas but had been spotted in the English Channel. The Tower on the Pike was built in 1733 and some of the stone used is thought to have come from the original beacon platform. It was a landowner's folly but now a popular magnet for locals who come to admire the views. The West Pennine Moors end and start at Rivington Pike. East of here, moorland hills interrupted by valleys, stretch all the way into Yorkshire. West of here, the edge falls away steeply and the West Lancashire Plain begins. You may well spot the lower heights of Parbold Hill and Ashurst Beacon looking west, but these do not interrupt the view to the coast and you should be able to see a prominent gasometer at Southport.

The boggy ascent from the Pike to the TV mast on Winter Hill is due to the rising of springs which form the infant River Douglas, a West Lancashire river that eventually flows into the Ribble Estuary. Modern masts started to appear on the summit of Winter Hill after the Second World War, it is obviously an ideal spot being the highest point on the West Pennine Moors. The magnificent TV mast is over 1,000 feet (303 metres) high. For the same reason, it attracted prehistoric man and excavations have revealed a Neolithic burial mound on Noon Hill and

Bronze Age cairns on Twa Lads Moor. Of further interest are two memorials on the summit of Winter Hill which record tragic events. The Scotsman's Stump was erected for James Henderson, a Scottish peddler who was shot dead whilst crossing the moor in 1803. On the wall of the transmitter station is a plaque erected by the Mayor of Douglas and the families of survivors of a fatal air crash on Winter Hill in February 1958. The plane was travelling from the Isle of Man to Manchester and the plaque carries the poignant message 'somewhere around the corner all is well'.

When the fine track leading down from Winter Hill meets the tarmac road, Coal Pit Road (it was an old route to moorland collieries) do not miss the 'Will Yo Come O' Sunday Morning?' memorial, the clarion cry which records the 1896 access battle won by 10,000 Boltonians who marched this way across the moor

Winter Hill Memorial

to reclaim an ancient right of way. Ironic that only a few years later on the other side of Winter Hill, the Bolton-born grocer who founded Port Sunlight and became Lord Leverhulme, granted a large tract of countryside for the recreation of the townsfolk – a true philanthropist!

The Route

1. Walk from the car park along the drive to the main entrance of Smithills Hall on Smithills Dean Road. Almost directly opposite on the far side of the road is a public footpath signpost pointing up a narrow ginnel between garden fences. Take this path, which soon crosses an estate road and continues straight ahead between fences to emerge at the top of a woodland sloping downhill. Continue straight ahead through the woodland along a cobbled track which swings sharply left and drops down to meet a lane alongside residen-

tial properties. Turn sharp right and follow the lane, crossing a brook and climbing uphill to a road junction below a tall chimney on the right restored by Bolton's celebrity steeplejack Fred Dibnah. Remember this Barrow Bridge mill chimney, as it will dominate the view for much of this walk. Turn right at the junction and follow Barrow Bridge Road slightly downhill for half a mile to reach pretty cottages lining the banks of a stream. Walk all the way through the hamlet until a car park is passed on the left and a gate is reached straight ahead when the lane kinks right over the stream.

2. Go through the spring gate and take the right (lower) path alongside the stream to a flight of steps leading up through woodland. Climb the 63 steps and continue uphill to go through a kissing gate. Continue straight ahead up the spur of the hill and the path soon forks. Take the left fork to a stile in a fence alongside a stream, Dakin's Brook. Cross the stile and follow the fenced path with the stream on the left. The path runs uphill for the next quarter of a mile to go through a kissing gate and meet a road. Look slightly to the left on the opposite side of the road to see a very narrow lane, signed as Matchmoor Lane, leading uphill behind a cottage. Join this lane and follow it as it zigzags uphill and soon reveals outstanding views looking back to Bolton, Manchester and the Pennines. Keep to the lane, ignoring footpath signs on either side, for half a mile until it turns sharp left at a crossroads of tracks.

3. Leave the lane here by continuing straight ahead along the farm track signposted for Slack Hall Farm. This meanders around the hillside to pass the farm on the left and reach gates. Go through the gate and continue straight ahead along the wide grass track with a wall to the left. Follow this track along the ridge, known as Burnt Edge, for nearly half a mile as it eventually swings right to reach gates at the head of a little valley (the same stream flows down to the cottages at Barrow Bridge). Go through the bridle gate to reach a waymarker signpost at a junction of paths. Turn left here and follow a distinct grass path, alongside a wall at first, through rough pasture. The view opens up looking westwards and a stile is soon reached that leads, surprisingly, onto a tarmac road. This is the access road to the TV transmitter station on Winter Hill and there is an information board marking the boundary of access land.

4. Turn right and follow the access road uphill for approximately 150 metres and look out for a passing place on the left-hand side of the

road next to a fenced off inlet of the North West Water Authority. Turn left here and follow a grass path downhill with a stream to the immediate right. The path heads directly for the Rivington reservoir in the valley below and soon crosses a brook and bears left to reach a gate. Go through the kissing gate and turn right to follow a wide stone road in the direction of the squat tower sat on top of Rivington Pike. This road, an old moorland highway from Bolton over to Belmont village, is followed in the direction of the Pike for the next mile and offers extensive views westwards across Lancashire. Bolton Wanderers fans will easily identify the space-age Reebok stadium close to the M61 close to the sprawl of Horwich, but also look out for Parbold Hill, the huge gasometer at Southport and Blackpool Tower. Keep to the road past the solitary Pike Cottage and the spur of Brown Hill and, when the road forks, keep to the right fork and soon you will see a stile on the right waymarked as a concessionary route to Rivington Pike, directly above.

5. Cross this stile and go directly up the steep slope through the small plantation to cross another stile. Continue straight up to reach the re-stored 18th century tower of Rivington Pike, from where there are views in all directions. The Pike stands at the western end of the spur of the Pennines which forms an arc above Greater Manchester and falls steeply away from here to the Lancashire Plain. Walk to the back of the tower and drop down to cross the ladder stile in a wooden fence. Look directly across to the Winter Hill masts and the route ahead can be seen as a distinct boggy path across open moorland to the tall TV mast. A compass may be required in poor weather. Follow this path, which becomes a long slog as the route meanders uphill through wet springs and the mast is, misleadingly, over a mile away. The springs mark the beginning of the infant River Douglas. The path eventually hits the access road just to the right of the transmitter station.

6. Turn left along the road if you wish to explore the interesting summit of Winter Hill. The highest point lies north of the TV transmitter station and is marked by a triangulation pillar between the line of smaller radio masts that overlook the hill's steep northern edge. A plaque to the 1958 air crash on Winter Hill has been placed on the wall of the transmitter station and, a bit further along the road, is Scotsman's Stump – the 19th century iron monument to the moorland murder of Scottish peddler, James Henderson. Looking south from the mast can be seen two tall stone cairns marking a Bronze Age

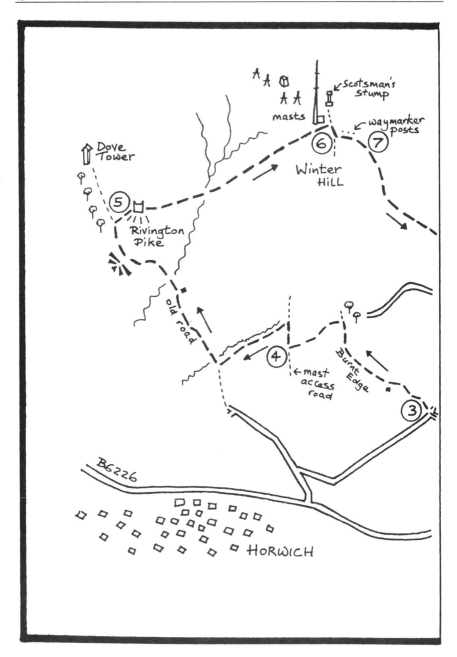

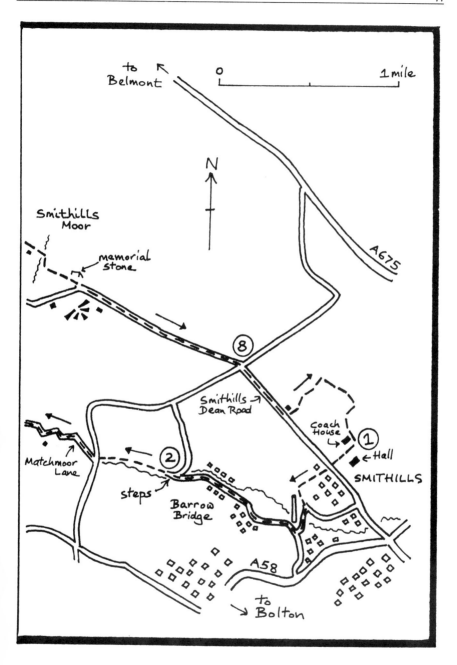

site on Twa Lads Moor. However, the walk continues by turning right onto the access road and walking just a few metres in the opposite direction to the transmitter station until a waymarker post is reached on the left-hand side of the road. Turn left and follow this path across a stile and along a well waymarked route (with Smithills Country Park yellow waymarkers) through a wall gap and across wooden platforms.

7. The path bears right after crossing the wooden platforms and picks up a distinct path through heather, across the moor in the direction of the Barrow Bridge chimney. Follow this meandering route, generally southeastwards, for the next mile and a quarter. Burnt Edge, the ridge followed earlier, comes into view over to the right and the path is eventually joined by a wall to the right and passes an abandoned shooting hut. It goes down and up steps above a little wooded valley then swings sharp left to follow a grass path alongside a wall. It meets a lane beyond a stile, alongside which is a 1996 memorial to the 10,000 Boltonians who marched along this path a century earlier to reclaim it as a right of way. It makes you proud to be walking it today! From this point there are excellent views looking south-east across the whole of Greater Manchester and of the West Pennines and Pennines encircling the city. Can you pick out Bolton Town Hall and the parish church amidst the sprawl? Cross the stile and walk straight ahead down the lane (known as Coal Pit Road) until it reaches a crossroads.

8. Take care and cross over to continue directly ahead down Smithills Dean Road, directly towards the centre of Bolton. Keep to the pavement for about half a mile until two right of way signposts are reached on either side of the road alongside a cottage (with an 1842 datestone) on the left. Turn left and follow the access road past the cottage until a brook is crossed next to a woodland on the left. After crossing the brook leave the access road by turning right opposite a cottage and heading slightly downhill to join a track leading to an old gate with a pedestrian access. Go through the gap and follow a woodland path which soon runs alongside a high walled enclosure to the left. The enclosure was formerly the garden centre of the Smithills complex and the path meets a track at the entrance to the site. Turn right and follow the track past Smithills Coaching House, a popular venue for Boltonian weddings. Continue right along the drive to reach Smithills Hall and car park.

2. Turton Moor and Turton Heights

This walk follows the shoreline of Entwistle Reservoir and passes through the pine plantations beyond its upper reaches to climb Turton Moor. A path skirts around the side of the moor and leads past ruined farmsteads before heading towards Delph Reservoir. From here the route climbs the steep shoulder of Turton Heights and crosses the bleak plateau before dropping down to pastures overlooking the Entwistle Valley. This walk can also be linked with Walk 3 (Cheetham Close) by a short section of path, providing an opportunity for a longer walk.

Peaks and Panoramas: TURTON MOOR and LONGWORTH MOOR form a large mass of rough pasture between the two A routes of Belmont Road and Blackburn Road. They are only half of a larger massif which continues north to Darwen Moor and Darwen Tower. Turton Moor has quite a hilly shape and has steep sides particularly on its west and east flanks, but the plateau gradually levels out at its highest point, not accessible by right of way. Almost exciting by comparison is TURTON HEIGHTS, a narrower ridge with steep sides that is separated from Turton Moor by a pass, through which Blackburn Road runs. Turton Heights is the northern end of the ridge which continues as a flat and featureless plateau to Cheetham Close (see Walk 3). There is little of interest on the summit of Turton Heights, all the excitement (namely, a triangulation pillar and stone circles) is on Cheetham Close. Still, the views from the flanks of Turton Moor and Turton Heights are far-reaching. Bolton, Manchester and the Pennines are visible from both as well as an excellent profile of Winter Hill to the west and Holcombe Moor to the east. The eastern slopes of Turton Heights also give a view north to Darwen, Blackburn, Longridge Fell and the hills of the Forest of Bowland in North Lancashire.

Distance: 7 miles

Map: Ordnance Survey Explorer 19: West Pennine Moors

Start: Entwistle Reservoir car parks, Batridge Road, off Greens Arms Road, Turton (Grid Reference 722 172).

Getting there: Entwistle reservoir is a popular honeypot and has two car parks, both accessible via different roads. It makes no difference which one you use (both are free!) as the walk can be started from either point. The lower car park, which has an information board, is reached by turning down Batridge Road which turns sharply off Greens Arms Road, the B6391, just north off Chapeltown village. If approaching from Chapeltown look for a turning on the right shortly after crossing over a railway bridge. The higher car park, above the dam, is known as the Batridge Barn car park and is reached by an access road approximately 500 metres further up Greens Arms Road after the turning for the lower car park. North West Water signs indicate the access road for Entwistle Reservoir.

Public transport: There is no direct bus service to Entwistle Reservoir but there is a rail connection nearby. Alight at Entwistle station on the Bolton-Blackburn line and follow the road leading downhill from the Strawbury Duck inn, past a row of railway cottages, to the reservoir dam. The starting point of the walk is on the far side of the dam. The return walk to and from the station will add a total of a mile to the walk length. Don't forget to check your train times though or you might be holed up at the Strawbury Duck all night (with a bit of luck).

Background

Entwistle reservoir was the first of the big reservoirs to be built in the Bradshaw Valley and construction began in 1831. It was built by bleachers to supply water to the valley's bleachworks but was compulsorily purchased by Bolton Corporation in 1863 to provide water to the town via a pipeline through Turton Heights. It still provides water to the town and has been planted up with conifers, giving it a fragrant flavour of the Scottish highlands although we are but five miles from Bolton town centre.

Bleaching dominated the moorland valleys in the 19th century whilst industrial activity also took place on the moors themselves since coal was to be found in 'them there hills'. One such colliery was to be found on Turton Moor and the walk briefly follows the line of an old tramway which led up to the disused shafts. The Turton Moor Colliery was actually still operating in the early years of the 20th century but an atmosphere of abandonment now pervades the moor with its ruined farmsteads and forgotten rights of way.

Turton and Longworth Moors are not exactly the Morecambe and Wise of the moorland world. They are far from entertaining and it is only the ruined farms that help the navigator to find a way across the bleak southern slopes. The farm known as Whewell's was the 17th century home of George Whewell, a man who executed the Earl of Derby in Bolton in 1651 following the Royalist defeat in the English Civil War. George Whewell's skull now resides in the Pack Horse Inn, Affetside (See Walk 4). Such ruins provide a contrast to the view that they offer to Manchester city centre, as these farms were a hive of activity when Manchester was just a small village.

Settlements of a much earlier age are also thought to have existed on the ridge of Turton Heights, which provided a rather flat plateau above the densely wooded valleys in prehistoric times. There is not much evidence of the ancient settlements today save for a few stones on Cheetham Close, passed on Walk 3.

The Walk

1. If parked on the lower car park, go through the gate on the opposite side of the lane; this marks the beginning of a shoreline path with the reservoir on your right. If parked on the higher car park, drop down the steps at the back of the car park to the same path slightly further up from the gate on the dam and turn left along it. The well-used and easy path between the water's edge and conifers is followed for almost a mile and heads towards conifer plantations behind which rises Turton Moor. The reservoir inlet is eventually reached and two wooden footbridges cross it, walk past the first but stop at the second one. The route heads up the wooden steps through the woodland on the left. If you wish to explore the upper reaches of the valley known as Yarnsdale, a permissive path can be followed which encircles both banks of the stream – this path is shown on the Ordnance Survey Explorer Map of the West Pennine Moors.

2. To continue the walk, turn left and climb the steps under the trees to a memorial bench on the right erected by the Bolton Group of the Holiday Fellowship. Behind it is a sign, also erected by the Holiday Fellowship, on which are written the words of a poetic 'request'. Continue straight ahead along the pleasant woodland path in a small clearing between the trees. When it joins a wide quarry track follow it straight ahead and pass under pylons. The roar of traffic becomes louder and busy Blackburn Road is soon reached by a gate and Peak and Northern sign. Turn right along the road and follow the pavement thankfully for only a very short distance (approximately 100 metres) until a Peak and Northern sign can be seen on the opposite side of the road. Cross the devil's road (the A666!) with care (you have walked under a great big sign warning cars about speeding!) and join this

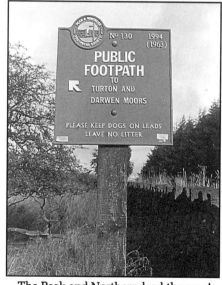

The Peak and Northern lead the way!

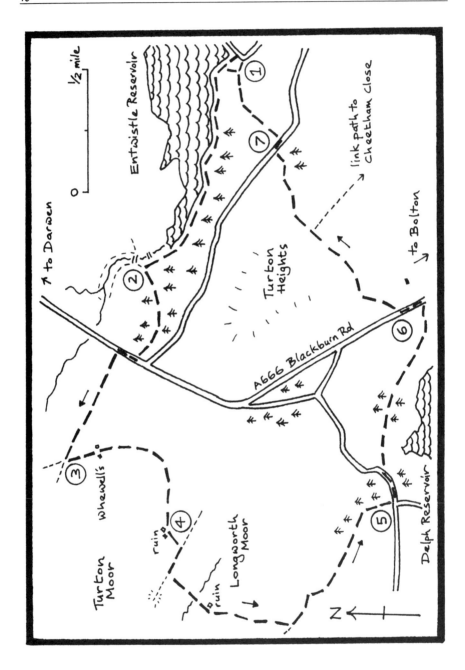

path, waymarked for Turton and Darwen Moors, over a stile. A distinct grassy track leads very gradually uphill heading for the right-hand side of Turton Moor. Follow it for approximately half a mile until another Peak and Northern signpost is reached at a junction of paths. The little valley over to the right forms the inlet to Entwistle Reservoir.

3. Take the path which turns sharp left off the track, heading for the solitary tree below the higher slopes of Turton Moor. The path is difficult to spot and appears to peter out in the rushes, but simply head for the tree, alongside which are walled remains of an old farmstead known as Whewell's. There are good views east to Peel Tower from here and also across to the ridge of Turton Heights on the other side of Blackburn Road. The path runs through the ruins and continue straight ahead, maintaining your height and following the line of a former wall boundary, now an earth mound. Cross the wall remains when they suddenly turn left and keep above the rushes to reach a stile in a wire fence. From here continue straight ahead along a faint path through rough pasture, maintaining the same height on the hillside. The view opens up south to Bolton and Manchester and over to the Pennines. The path changes direction as it bears right around the side of the moor and heads towards Winter Hill. Unfortunately in the middle of this bleak pasture the path seems to disappear completely! You are aiming for the substantial farm ruin, complete with its windows, which can be seen straight ahead. A faint track runs alongside the wall just above you, from which you can drop down to reach the ruin through two gateposts.

4. Walk to the lower side of the main ruin where it abuts onto a wall running straight down the hill. From here, a boggy path through thick rushes can be picked out which heads diagonally down to a stream crossing, roughly in the direction of the Winter Hill masts. The path then meets a distinct track running left to right – an old colliery incline. Turn right along this and follow it for approximately 120 metres, before bearing off it to the left below some old mine heaps and fenced off shafts. Unfortunately, the circumnavigation of Longworth Moor does not get any easier and the best thing to do is to continue to aim for the Winter Hill masts until a stream is crossed and a track on the far side of the stream leads up to yet another ruined farmhouse. From here, at last, a distinct boggy track can be followed straight ahead to reach an adjoining stone track

approximately quarter of a mile away. Turn left and follow this wide farm track gradually downhill for approximately three-quarters of a mile until it meets a lane. The track passes through gates and then runs alongside a conifer plantation before the lane is reached at a stile and gate.

5. Turn left along the lane for approximately 180 metres until a foot-path signpost on the right is reached as the lane starts to bend. Go through the gate and look above the trees to the top of Turton Heights, which remains to be climbed. The boggy path drops down to a footbridge in a meadow and then bear right and climb up the other side to a gate and stile at the edge of a plantation. Follow the stony track through the plantation and, at the far end, cross the stile onto a grassy track overlooking Delph Reservoir. Follow this track above the reservoir to reach another gate and stile where it forks. Keep left and the track runs between walls and soon meets Blackburn Road again. Cross the road with care, turning left and fol-lowing the pavement for approximately 150 metres until a footpath signpost is reached on the right where there is a stile in a wall gap. The quick ascent of Turton Heights is about to begin.

6. Cross the stile and climb uphill, bearing left to reach the wall-side at the back of the plantation on the left. Follow the wall-side up to the top of the hill to reach a gate. Go through the gate and turn left to reach a stile in the next fence boundary. Cross this and take the path waymarked to the right which climbs straight up the side of the moor. The path is easy to follow and ascends steeply before soon lev-elling out as the flatter top of the plateau is reached. There are good views along the ridge, to Bolton and Manchester and also back to Delph Reservoir and Winter Hill. On the top of the plateau, there are no features, the highest point of the moor lies to the left and Cheetham Close (see Walk 3) lies to the right. A faint path leading sharp right from the main path over the hill can take you along the ridge to the triangulation pillar on Cheetham Close, providing a link with Walk 3. But to continue this walk keep going straight ahead and the path begins to drop down the far side of the ridge. The view opens out to Entwistle Reservoir and north to Blackburn and the For-est of Bowland. Pass a solitary hawthorn tree to reach a stile in the fence. Cross this and walk under the pylons, heading diagonally right downhill to reach the bottom corner of the conifer plantation on your right. Cross the stile in the field corner.

7. Turn right on the road and follow it for approximately 200 metres until a footpath signpost is reached on the left by a stile and gate. Join this path and head downhill along the wall-side until a waymarker post is reached by the wall on the left. Bear right here, leaving the wall and heading diagonally across the field to reach a stile in a fence onto the higher car park. If you are parked on the lower car park either drop down the steps to rejoin the reservoir path and follow it back to the kissing gate or walk through the higher car park to reach another set of steps, down a grass bank to the road by the lower car park.

3. Cheetham Close

This walk follows the edge of Jumbles Reservoir and climbs to moorland beyond historic Turton Tower, before descending to Turton village and following the riverside and reservoir path south through the wooded valley of the
Bradshaw Brook. It also links with Walk 2 (Turton Moor and Heights) and
Walk 4 (Affetside) allowing opportunities for longer walks.

Peaks and Panoramas: The steep-sided ridge running between TURTON
HEIGHTS and CHEETHAM CLOSE is climbed, with the south-facing spur of
Cheetham Close giving the best views across the West Pennines and towards Bolton and Manchester. The summit has a triangulation pillar and the
scattered remains of ancient stone circles.

Distance: 7 miles

Map: Ordnance Survey Explorer Sheet No. 19 West Pennine Moors.

Start: Jumbles Country Park car park, off Bradshaw Road, Bradshaw,
Bolton (Grid Reference 736 139).

Getting there: Jumbles Country Park is signposted on the left-hand side of
the A676 Bradshaw Road running north from Bolton towards Hawkshaw and
Ramsbottom. Follow the lane leading down off the main road and turn left at
the end for the toilets and car park. A visitor centre overlooking the Jumbles
Reservoir is on the other side of the access lane.

Public transport: Buses between Bolton and Edgworth stop at Bromley
Cross train station and along Chapeltown Road and both are convenient for
a short walk downhill, via Ousel Nest Meadows, to cross the footbridge over
the dam of Jumbles Reservoir and climb the steps to the car park.

Jumbles Country Park is also accessible by train. Alight at Bromley Cross
station on the Bolton-Blackburn line (bus travellers can also alight here) and
follow Grange Road for approximately a quarter of a mile until a footpath
through Ousel Nest Meadows is reached on the right-hand side of the road
through a gate. The path leads downhill to a footbridge over the reservoir outlet and climbs the steps to the car park. In total, the return walk to and from
the station will add approximately one and a half miles to the total route
above.

Background

Jumbles Reservoir is one of three reservoirs created in the valley of the
Bradshaw Brook which flows southwards from the West Pennine
Moors and is the major tributary of the River Croal near Bolton town

The waterwheel at Black Rock Mill

centre. In the 18th and 19th centuries, Bradshaw Brook became a site for fulling mills and bleachworks associated with the textile industry and the Entwistle Reservoir (1831) and Wayoh Reservoir (1876) were built to maintain a constant water supply for the bleaching industry. These two reservoirs are further up the valley from Jumbles and now supply drinking water to Bolton, whilst Jumbles itself was only opened in 1971 as a compensation reservoir. In the flooded valley once stood Horrobin Mill, a bleachworks that lasted from the 1780s up until 1941 whilst, further up the valley, at Turton Bottoms, stood Black Rock Mill (see also Walk 4) which has also been demolished. Its restored water wheel stands in the grounds of Turton Tower and is passed on the walk.

Turton Tower is a fine Tudor house added to a 15th century pele tower, probably built by the lord of Turton manor as a defence against possible Scottish invaders. Over six centuries it has been owned by some of the most famous family names in Lancashire history – the Lathoms owned the site as early as 1212 but it was the Tarbocks of Merseyside who built the original tower. Perhaps they were the ancestors of Scouser comedian, Jimmy Tarbuck! The property then passed to the Orrells of Wigan who built most of the present house and then to the Manchester cloth merchant, Humphrey Chetham. A rare thing in the

17th century, Chetham was a self-made man who bought his way into the landed gentry. In the 19th century, the tower was owned by another textile magnate, James Kay. The line of the Bolton-Blackburn railway cut through the grounds of the estate in 1848 and steam trains must have given the Kay family many a sleepless night in the days before double glazing. Still they did manage to get a nice railway bridge out of it and the mock castellated structure is passed over on the walk.

Humphrey Chetham (1580-1653) was the founder of Manchester's famous Chetham's School and Library and he obviously was to wield some influence in the Turton area. Even though he did not live at Turton Tower, not even as a holiday home, he did manage to get the local pub and hill named after him – the Chethams Arms and Cheetham Close. Cheetham Close is the partly wooded spur overlooking Egerton, Toppings and Bromley Cross and is the continuation of a rather dull ridge from Turton Heights (see also Walk 2). It looks more exciting on the O.S. map which records on the summit the words 'Stone Circles' in ancient lettering. Stones can still be found on the north side of the triangulation pillar on Chetham Close, but they have been much disturbed and new cairn circles have also been created by many a disappointed rambler. However, the original stones suggested the existence of a Bronze Age settlement on top of the moor. It was probably a high clearing above a valley that was then heavily forested.

The Route

1. Head for the corner of the car park at the opposite end to the toilets and join a path downhill, via steps, to woodland below the high dam at the southern end of Jumbles Reservoir. A footbridge across the Bradshaw Brook is reached below the dam wall, cross this and take the path forking left on the far side of the bridge, uphill to enter a large meadow which has been recently planted with trees. Follow the main path through the meadow, passing gardens on the right and a picnic area on the left until it reaches a kissing gate onto a lane.

2. Turn right and follow the wide lane below trees until Grange Farm is reached on the right. Continue straight ahead along the track that passes between stable blocks and leads to a kissing gate at the edge of woodland. Go through the kissing gate and follow the path through the trees along the reservoir edge for the next quarter of a mile to cross a footbridge at an inlet to Jumbles Reservoir. Turn right almost

immediately when the path meets a lane and follow the lane down to a car park overlooking the reservoir. At the rear of the car park the path passes between a small fishing reservoir and cottages and continues close to the water's edge until a wide bridge across Jumbles is reached to the right. Turn sharp left here next to the bridge to follow the grass path uphill via steps waymarked by a Peak and Northern signpost. The path climbs through woodland and bears right to a stile. Cross the stile and follow the field edge downhill, passing a concrete pill box on the left, to meet a road.

3. Turn sharp left and follow the pavement along the road (between Bolton and Turton) uphill for approximately 250 metres. The driveway entrance to Turton Tower is then reached on the right. Turn right into the drive and the gates of the historic property are soon passed on the right; the Tower can be glimpsed through the trees. Continue straight ahead and the restored water wheel from Turton's Black Rock Mill is also passed on the same side. Continue along the track, then cross the Bolton-Blackburn railway via a splendid castellated bridge complete with its own turrets. The wide stone track then bears right and climbs alongside a wooded stream to meet another track running from left to right. Fork right here and go through the kissing gate to join a farm track with a wall on the right. This farm track is followed, gradually uphill, for the next mile and a quarter, passing Clough House Farm on the right, until it meets a road. There are fine views looking right to the Bradshaw Valley, Turton, Edgworth and beyond to the Peel Monument on the spur of Holcombe Moor.

4. When the gateway leading out onto the road is finally reached, look for the footpath sign on the left and follow this over the stile in the fence and follow the grass path uphill between fences. Cross another stile and follow the sunken path between mound-like hills marked on the map as 'Three Lowes'. The path bears slightly left, then right around the hillside and heads for the pylons directly ahead across boggy ground. Cross under the pylons and bear right to meet a moorland wall. Cross the stile in the right-hand corner of the wall and follow the distinct path which swings left and climbs gradually away from the wall and runs diagonally up the hillside. The path then runs alongside the remains of a wall boundary on the right and levels out onto a moorland plateau. Continue straight ahead to reach the top of the plateau at a crossroads of paths close to an old Bolton Cor-

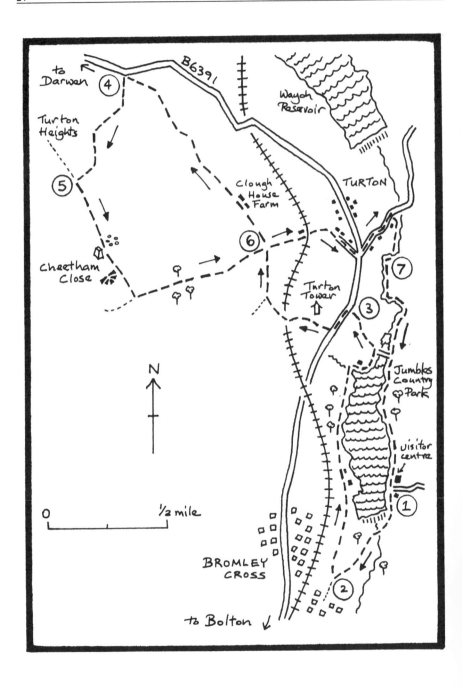

poration Waterworks Boundary marker. To the right, the featureless ridge runs to the summit of Turton Heights and the moorland continues several miles north to Darwen Tower and beyond. The massif of Winter Hill lies to the west.

5. Turn sharp left by the Waterworks Boundary marker and climb up the well-used path through a gap in the wall to reach the summit of Cheetham Close. There is a triangulation pillar here and the difficult-to-find remains of ancient stone circles on the north side of the summit, not to be confused with a number of fake 'modern' cairns. Follow the path straight ahead from the summit to drop down to a stile and gate in the corner of a wall on the left. The view opens up, looking south towards Turton golf course, Bolton and Manchester. Turn left, cross the stile and head downhill towards woodland and the steeple of Turton church. Cross the stile in the fence into the woodland and go straight through the woodland to cross another stile on the far side of the trees. Go directly downhill to another stile and continue straight ahead, passing a pond on the left and crossing under pylons, to rejoin the farm track followed earlier.

6. Cross over the stile in the wall facing you and follow the grassy path to keep above the steep sided valley to the left. The path drops down to a gate alongside a mill and leads to a level crossing over the railway line. Turton train station once stood on the far side of the line here. Take care and cross the railway to follow the cobbled lane downhill. Soon, where the road forks, take the right fork and follow the lane past houses, including one interestingly converted from the village bank, to reach a road junction. Take care and cross the busy Bolton-Turton road to join the lower road, Wellington Road, signposted for Edgworth, Entwistle and Bury. Keep to the right-hand side of this road and follow it downhill for nearly a quarter of a mile. Shortly, after a public footpath signpost is passed on the opposite side of the road, look out for a footpath on the right. Take this cobbled path which drops steeply down from the road to houses. Turn right at the bottom of the hill and follow the lane which crosses a bridge over the Bradshaw Brook. Immediately after crossing the bridge, turn sharp right to join a path, with the brook immediately on the right.

7. Follow this riverside path past pretty cottages and through woodland for the next half mile until the northern end of Jumbles Reser-

voir is reached at a wide footbridge. Do not cross the bridge but continue straight ahead along the reservoir edge keeping the reservoir to your right. This popular path is followed for the next half a mile and leads to the country park visitor centre at the southern end of Jumbles. Continue straight ahead past the visitor centre to reach the car park.

4. Affetside

This walk follows the Bradshaw Valley upstream beyond Jumbles Reservoir and climbs through pastures overlooked by high moors to the north of Hawkshaw village. It then meanders through a hidden valley before climbing up to the route of a Roman road which leads to the isolated hamlet of Affetside. An old track down the western slopes of Affetside, giving fine views westward, then leads back down to the Jumbles valley. It also links with Walk 3 (Cheetham Close) giving an opportunity for a longer walk.

Peaks and Panoramas: AFFETSIDE is a tiny linear settlement along the route of a Roman road and gives its name to the perfectly shaped hill on which it is situated. This relatively broad but low hill has at its highest point a Headless Cross and the Pack Horse Inn but the most extensive views are to be found lower down its slopes. Its western side looks all the way from Manchester, north through Bolton to Winter Hill, Cheetham Close, Turton Moor to Darwen Tower. Its southern and eastern aspects look towards Holcombe Moor and Bury and stretches over much of Greater Manchester, the Rossendale Fells and the Pennines. A little hill with a big, big view!

Distance: 7½ miles

Map: Ordnance Survey Explorer Sheet No. 19 West Pennine Moors

Start: Jumbles Country Park car park, off Bradshaw Road, Bradshaw, Bolton (Grid Reference 736 139).

Getting there: Jumbles Country Park is signposted on the left-hand side of the A676 Bradshaw Road running north from Bolton to Hawkshaw and Ramsbottom. If approaching from Bolton town centre, turn left at the junction by the Crofter's Arms. The turning for Jumbles is about a mile and a quarter up the Bradshaw Road. Follow the reservoir access road, which has speed bumps, leading down off the main road and turn left at the end for the toilets and large car park. A visitor centre overlooking Jumbles is on the other side of the access road.

Public transport: Buses between Bolton and Edgworth stop at Bromley Cross train station and along Chapeltown Road and both are convenient for a short walk downhill, via Ousel Nest Meadows, to cross the footbridge over the dam of Jumbles Reservoir and climb the steps to the car park. Jumbles Country Park is also accessible by **train**. Alight at Bromley Cross station on the Bolton-Blackburn line (bus travellers can also alight here) and follow Grange Road for approximately quarter of a mile until a footpath through Ousel Nest Meadows is reached on the right-hand side of the road through a gate. The path leads downhill to a footbridge over the reservoir outlet and climbs the steps to the car park. In total, the return walk to and from the station will add approximately one and a half miles to the total walk route above.

Background

The site of Horrobin Mill bleach works lies beneath the waters of Jumbles Reservoir and, winding your way up the Bradshaw Valley to Turton Bottoms, the site of another bleach works, Black Rock Mill, has also disappeared. Exclusive new detached houses have replaced it on the banks of the brook, but the pretty mill cottages along cobbled Birch Road remain and the old water wheel has found its way to the grounds of Turton Tower (see Walk 3). A surviving tall chimney, stuck in the bottom of a field above the brook, is the most visible remnant of the 19th century industry that once thrived in the valley. It was built so high to carry the smoke away from the fields where cloth was left out to dry in the sun. The settlement of Hawkshaw had a similar history of bleaching and dyeing based upon local springs, including a mill down Two Brooks Lane. Most of the village's fine 19th century buildings survive and are becoming desirable residences, as Hawkshaw's potential as a pleasant commuter settlement has been realised.

Many surviving farmsteads on the moors around Hawkshaw have 16th and 17th century datestones but the oldest thing hereabouts, possibly dating from 79 AD, is the line of a Roman road from Manchester (Mamucium) to Ribchester (Bremetennacum) in Lancashire north of the River Ribble. This important line of communication, the main Roman highway west of the Pennines, continued north to Carlisle and Hadrian's Wall. The Romans were renowned for the straightness of their roads – they followed a direct line between the forts at Manchester and Ribchester and did not worry if it meant crossing high ground. The line of the road has been largely lost in the urban sprawl of Manchester and Blackburn, so it is nice to see it preserved in tarmac on the moorland at Affetside and also a few miles north at Edgworth.

The road remained a useful trading highway across the moors at least between Manchester and Blackburn long after the Romans debunked in the 5th century AD. The name of the roadside inn, the Pack Horse, at Affetside is testament to this. The inn actually dates from 1443 and housed an ancient well. In the bar of the Pack Horse there is a curious artefact – the skull of executioner George Whewell. In 1651, he chopped off the head of the 7th Earl of Derby in Bolton for fighting Lancashire's Royalist cause in the English Civil War. Whewell lived at a farm on Turton Moor, the ruins of which are visited in Walk 2. Antiquities abound here, for Affetside also has the remains of a wayside cross, now designated as an Ancient Monument. The date of the cross is unknown but it probably indicates the site where a market was held in days of yore.

The Route

1. From the car park, walk back to the toilets and continue straight ahead to reach information boards and the visitor centre on the right, overlooking Jumbles Reservoir. Continue straight ahead along the wide track which clings to the reservoir edge for the next half mile. The route is well-used and is popular with dog walkers. Along the way a bridge is crossed, a good place for heron spotting, and the track runs through woodland, eventually to reach a wide bridge with blue railings crossing the reservoir to the left. Do not cross this bridge but instead, continue straight ahead beyond the top of the reservoir to follow the right-hand bank of the inlet stream, Bradshaw Brook. This pleasant path meanders through woodland alongside the stream for over half a mile until, shortly after passing some pretty cottages, it reaches an old packhorse bridge on the left, adjacent to a new residential development to your right.

2. Do not cross this bridge but continue straight ahead, keeping the stream on your immediate left and going up and down some stone steps with the fenced garden of a new residential property immediately to your right. The distinct path then climbs through woodland up the steep valley slope and leaves the stream behind for the moment. At the top of the woodland, the path leads out to a stony track running left to right. Turn left and follow this downhill, going through a metal gate and passing a cottage on the left. The track drops down to a row of cottages signed as Birches Road. This road swings around to the left but do not follow it. Instead, follow another old track on the right with a wooden gate across it. Turn right here (opposite the Birches Road sign above the corner cottage) and go through the gap next to the gate. The track swings back on itself and meets a tarmac driveway. Turn right onto this drive and follow it around to some modern residential properties until a gate and stone steps to your left are reached.

3. Climb the stone staircase on the left and go through the latch gate at the top. Follow the line of paved flags up through the field alongside a wire fence. A tall chimney (high enough to have once taken smoke out of the valley) is passed in the field to the left and the path simply keeps alongside the wire fence and follows it uphill to a cottage. Cross the stiles near the top of the hill and continue straight ahead along the edge of the private lawn and neat cobbled patio to reach the

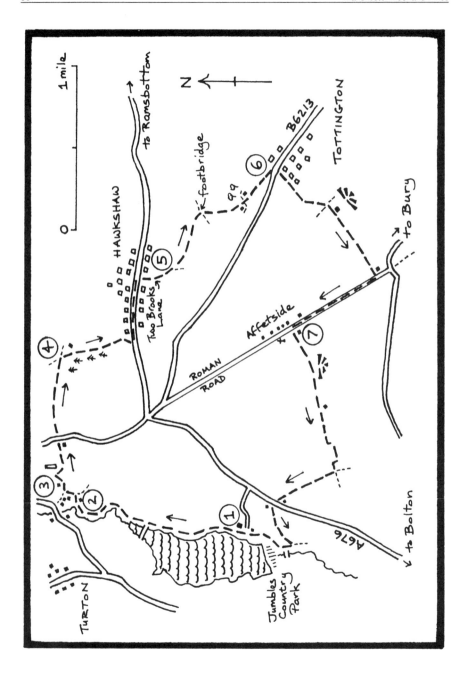

road by the side of the property, Pallet Farm Cottage. Cross the road and, slightly to the right, join the farm track opposite and follow this uphill alongside a wall. The track swings sharp left at the top of the field and heads for the farm. Leave the track here, go through the open gateway and continue almost directly ahead to a little metal gate in a gap in the boundary wall. There are good views back to Edgworth, Turton and an impressive railway viaduct on the Bolton-Blackburn line. Cross the next field, aiming slightly right and, at the top of the hill, a stile in the next boundary wall will be spotted. Continue straight ahead to an obvious stile at the next boundary and, beyond this, cross two stiles at the far end of the next field. After crossing these, follow a diagonal line uphill through the grass field to reach a gate by the edge of a conifer plantation.

4. Go through the gate to join a track alongside the trees. Turn left and follow this downhill to join a tarmac access road leading from the nearby farm. Turn right along this and follow it downhill between the trees. This access road is followed downhill beyond the plantation and offers excellent views from nearby Hawkshaw to the Peel Tower, Knowl Hill and across the whole of North Manchester to the Pennines (look for the radio mast on Windy Hill!). In the wall to your right, at the end of the plantation, there is a memorial to Margaret and William Short. The access road eventually swings right and joins the A676 Bolton-Ramsbottom road. Turn left and follow the pavement to Hawkshaw village. Walk along this main road for about a quarter of a mile until a lane signed Two Brooks Lane is reached on the right. This is after the village store is passed and just before the Wagon and Horses pub on the left-hand side of the road.

5. Turn right down Two Brooks Lane which soon becomes a wide track beneath trees and leads past tennis courts on the left. Be alert after passing the tennis courts as you need to pick up a distinct path which forks off to the left (by a drain cover) when the main track kinks slightly right and runs downhill. Take this narrower path which runs under trees and drops downhill, eventually to reach a ladder stile in a wall. Cross this and continue straight ahead, heading for the fence and stream bank on the right of the field and following this to a stile and wooden footbridge at the next boundary. Cross these and turn sharp left from the bridge to pick up a distinct grass path which bears right under trees. The path goes through a lush meadow surrounded by steep valley sides and reaches a waymarked

footbridge. Cross this and continue in the same direction to a wood-land and cottages. Follow the track between a wooden fence and out-building, bear right around the pretty cottage directly ahead and follow the main driveway straight ahead with the cottage and hedge to the left. The tarmac drive passes through a stile and gate and runs uphill for a third of a mile to reach a road at a stile and gate.

6. Cross the road (Turton Road, leading from Bury) and, directly oppo-site, take the signed footpath uphill alongside a house (number 145). You are now on the edge of residential Tottington and the path runs uphill alongside garden fences, crosses a lane and continues straight ahead up a drive to Clay Brook Farm. Go through the waymarked gate straight ahead when the drive swings right to the farm. The path follows the hedge side and crosses a stile at the top of the field to meet a crossroads of tracks. Continue straight ahead up the drive to Sheep Hill and follow the waymarked route around the right of the property, avoiding the garden. The path then follows a boggy path between wire fences and crosses stiles to follow a wet field edge up-hill alongside a wire fence. There are good views south to central Manchester and the Pennines from here. Keep the fence on your im-mediate left and the path eventually joins a lane over a stile adjacent to a cottage. The lane is the route of the Roman road from Manches-ter to Ribchester. Look left for a partial view of central Manchester less than 12 miles away, straight down the hill. Turn right and follow the moorland highway in the footsteps of Roman soldiers, gradually uphill to the higher ground where the lonely cottages of Affetside are found.

7. After passing the Pack Horse Inn on the right, look for a path leaving on the left-hand side of the road to the right of a bungalow. Before joining this, you may wish to view the Headless Cross, a bit further up the lane on the left. Return to the path between the cross and the Inn and follow it over manicured lawns to a step in a wall straight ahead. The path then runs downhill, roughly under the line of tele-graph poles, to another stile then down a grass path to cross another stile by a house. The view opens out – particularly westward – taking in Bolton, Winter Hill, Cheetham Close, Turton Heights, Turton Moor and north to Darwen Tower. The path continues in the same direction along a track which kinks around the railings of a water works. At the lower end of the railings, almost immediately cross a stile in the fence on the right. The path crosses a little brook to follow

The view to Cheetham Close

a field edge, with the fence on the right, to another stile. Continue straight ahead down the drive to meet the main road (from Bolton to Ramsbottom), and directly opposite cross several stiles which lead downhill along a waymarked field-edge path to enter a woodland with a stream on the left. This quickly meets another path running left to right, turn right and follow this to meet another track by a brown Croal-Irwell Valley sign. Turn right and climb wooden steps uphill to emerge in a corner of the Jumbles car park.

5. Holcombe Moor

This walk follows a farm track around the lower slopes of Holcombe Moor before climbing up the high valley of Red Brook and crossing the moor to view the lonely monuments of the Pilgrim's Stone and the Ellen Strange memorial. It then follows an old moorland highway that once linked Rossendale with Bury and climbs the moor again to reach the top of Harcles Hill and take in the magnificent panoramic views from the popular Peel Tower.

Peaks and Panoramas: HOLCOMBE MOOR is a vast expanse of moorland overlooking Ramsbottom and most of it now lies in the ownership of the National Trust. Its most distinctive feature is the steep sided spur stretching south upon which stands the high brick monument of the Peel Tower which offers possibly the best views across Greater Manchester to be found in this book. The panorama from here takes in the whole of the West Pennines and the Pennines and particularly towns such as Ramsbottom, Heywood, Bury and the city centre. The highest point of Holcombe Moor is BULL HILL which has a triangulation pillar but lies within Ministry of Defence firing ranges. The moor also rises to the stepped plateau of HARCLES HILL which offers views north and east to the Irwell Valley and Rossendale hills. Looking north from here on a clear day also reveals Pendle Hill and, possibly, Penyghent and Ingleborough in the Yorkshire Dales.

Distance: 6 miles

Map: Ordnance Survey Explorer No. 19 West Pennine Moors

Start: Peel Tower public car park, Lumb Carr Road, Holcombe, Ramsbottom (Grid Reference 782 163).

Getting there: This car park is situated upon the B6214 Holcombe Brook-Haslingden Road and lies between the road junction at Holcombe Brook and Holcombe village further up the hill. If approaching from the Holcombe Brook junction, continue straight up the hill past the Hare and Hounds pub and the car park is on the right and is signposted from the road with a brown tourist sign for the Peel Tower.

Public transport: A bus service between Bury and Rawtenstall stops on the hill of Lumb Carr Road close to the Peel Tower car park between Holcombe Brook and Holcombe village. It is just as easy to alight at the Shoulder of Mutton pub in Holcombe village and opposite it join Cross Lane, following it southwards for about 300 metres to pick up the walk route.

Background

Standing 112 feet (34 metres) high on the edge of Holcombe Moor, the Peel Tower is the most identifiable landmark of the West Pennines and from almost any part of the northern half of Greater Manchester it can be seen standing guard on a steep-sided spur overlooking the middle reaches of the Irwell Valley. The Tower was opened in 1852 and celebrates the Repeal of the Corn Laws by the then prime minister, Robert Peel, who was born in nearby Bury to the son of a textile manufacturer. The Corn Laws had kept grain prices and, therefore, bread prices high throughout the early 19th century and abolishing them was obviously popular amongst Bury folk who wished to commemorate their most famous son – who also founded the police force. A modern-day equivalent would probably be if Mrs. Thatcher had repealed the poll tax and the people of Grantham erected a monument to her. But, of course, she never did. The Tower was built from local millstone grit, hence the quarried holes surrounding it, and has now apparently reopened to the public – but I have yet to see it open.

The Peel Tower is a relative newcomer to Holcombe Moor, which takes its name from the old village which nestles beneath its stark shoulder. The moor is a southern spur of the Rossendale Uplands and

The Peel Tower, overlooking the city.

in ancient times pilgrims travelling to and from Whalley Abbey in Lancashire crossed the moor and prayed and rested by a cross that is known to have existed here at least as early as 1176. The site of the cross is recorded by the present-day square stone which stands on the flat plateau and was erected in 1902 by the lord of the manor. The base of the original cross was removed in 1901 by some Edwardian vandals – even in those days you couldn't keep anything unless it was nailed down! Was it sold at some horse and trap boot sale? The present stone monument came from a local quarry and was carted up from Ramsbottom railway yard by horses. Even further back in time, Bull Hill was believed to be a prehistoric site as stone tool fragments were found on its summit.

Pilgrims were replaced by textile merchants and part of this walk follows a farm track, Moor Road, running north-south along the edge of the moor which was once an important highway between Bury, Haslingden and Clitheroe. Such routes kept high to avoid boggy valleys and also, in this case, to avoid the restricted entry of the Forest of Rossendale which extended down to Holcombe. Not far from this old highway is the resting place of Ellen Strange, a local girl and 'hapless maid' who was murdered on the moor and is remembered by a stone pillar and cross. The cairn of stones placed on her resting place is even marked on old 1840s maps. More modern highways, such as the M66, follow the floor of the Irwell Valley, which was formed by a geological fault known as the Ramsbottom fault.

The National Trust has had an interest in this area since 1943 when it acquired the Stubbins estate on the western slopes above the Irwell from a Colonel Porritt. It acquired Holcombe Moor in 1994 from the Ministry of Defence and this was definitely good news for ramblers. But military rifle ranges are still to be found around Bull Hill and the Red Brook valley and you will get a view of the army assault course which was once the star of ITV's 'The Krypton Factor'. Like Stone Age man, religious pilgrims, Ellen Strange and Bobby Peel, Gordon Burns is now just another ghost of Holcombe Moor.

The Route

1. From the car park entrance, cross the road and go through a gate, almost opposite. Follow a permissive path uphill between a wall and fence to reach another gate. Turn right on the cobbled road,

Holcombe Old Road, and follow this for only a short distance before turning sharp left up the hill on the route signed as a private road. Ignore the path swinging right – keep left on the farm road alongside a wall. Already there are fine views looking south and east. The walled farm road is followed for about one and a half miles along the boundary between fields and unenclosed moorland. Not surprisingly, it is known as Moorbottom Road. The route swings around the hillside and after passing Bank Top Farm the road becomes stonier and crosses stiles by gates before forking into two. Look left for a south-north view of Affetside, Winter Hill, Cheetham Close, Turton Heights, Turton Moor and Darwen Tower. You will also see the Ministry of Defence training area in the valley below, including the army assault course once used on Granada's TV quiz, 'The Krypton Factor'. Keep to the right fork and the track rises gradually along the hillside to meet three warning signs and a flag at the edge of firing ranges.

2. Be aware of the proximity of the military firing ranges, particularly if red flags are flying to indicate shooting activity. However, the route takes the right fork and finally starts to climb uphill. There is an excellent view left to the dramatic hanging valley of Red Brook, which tumbles down from a high escarpment. One could almost be in the Lake District mountains when you look at this view – not four miles north of Bury! Follow the distinct path uphill, keeping the line of marker posts and warning signs on the left. The path levels out onto a featureless moorland plateau and the range boundary markers lead you straight to the prominent Pilgrim Stone, which stands at a crossroads of paths. The detailed inscriptions on the four faces of the monument outline why it is here. It was erected in 1902 to replace the ancient Pilgrims' Cross, which stood here at least as early as 1176. Flat, featureless Holcombe Moor surrounds you and reaches its highest point at Bull Hill to the north-west. A path, striking left from the monument, leads up to the summit of Bull Hill if you wish to 'bag' it, but take heed of flying red flags, as the area lies within the army ranges.

3. To continue the walk, follow the distinct path which continues ahead in the same direction you ascended the moor. Rossendale and, possibly, views of Pendle Hill and Penyghent lie to the north. The path skirts over the slope below Bull Hill and heads downhill keeping the range boundary markers to the immediate left. Look

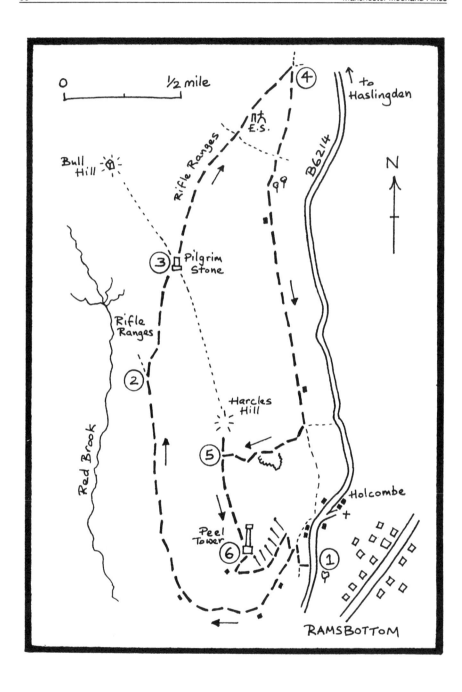

back to the broad expanse of Holcombe Moor and below is the deep cutting of the Irwell Valley through which the M66 runs. On the opposite side of the valley the hills of Scout Moor and Whittle Pike rise, dissected by wooded Dearden Clough and vast quarries. Follow the path down to where it forks close to three signs, which indicate the edge of the range. Keep to the left fork which continues across the moor (the right fork drops down to a wall corner) and the boggy path through rough pasture veers slightly right and skirts the corner of a derelict wall. Just after the wall, you pass on the right a cross in a cairn and a spooky stone pillar inscribed with the initials 'E.S.' – which indicate the spot where Ellen Strange was murdered. The path continues downhill and veers right to become a sunken path running parallel with a wall on the left. At the bottom of the hill, the path reaches two gates in wall boundaries next to a National Trust signpost.

4. Do not go through either of the gates but say ta-ta to Haslingden and the view of Rossendale and turn sharp right to follow the farm track heading south towards Greater Manchester. This farm track, Moor Road, is followed for the next mile and a half running parallel to the B road, M66 and the Irwell Valley below to your left. Keep the wall to the left and head back in the direction of the Peel Tower. The track passes a woodland on the left, a farm on the right and goes through a gate to continue to a farm on the left of the track. Shortly after passing the second farm the track meets a tarmac road which heads up the hillside to the right. At this point, head for the bench on the right and turn right along a stone track, which leads uphill and swings left. When the track soon forks, take the right fork which follows a grass path uphill to a disused quarry. The path goes under telegraph poles and goes into the quarry before veering right at the back of it and running alongside a wall. The distinct path runs up the right-hand side of a brook to reach the bottom of a steep slope where it meets a path coming down the steep slope of Harcles Hill.

5. Turn right and climb the slope directly uphill to Harcles Hill where the views north are regained. The view east across the Irwell Valley takes in Scout Moor, Dearden Clough, Whittle Pike and Knowl Hill. To continue the walk drop back down to the path crossroads, cross the brook and continue directly ahead towards Peel Tower. Climb gradually uphill, go through two gates to reach the towering Victorian monument. It is 112 feet (34 metres) high but its moorland base alone commands views from the Pennines across the Cheshire Plain to North Wales and the Lancashire coast. Much nearer are the steeple of Holcombe church, Nuttall, Holcombe Brook and Bolton, Bury and Manchester. Enjoy the view!

6. Join the stone track below Peel Tower and turn right along it, heading downhill to a farmhouse. Keep to the main track which zigzags sharp left and descends the steep spur, turning sharp right to join the track followed at the start of this walk. Turn left, then right to rejoin the cobbled lane and leave this shortly on the right, following the permissive path, which leads downhill to the car park on the opposite side of the road.

6. Knowl Hill and Scout Moor

This walk explores the lonely moors north of Ashworth Moor Reservoir, starting with a short but steep climb up to the distinctive Knowl Hill and then a
trudge across a boggy plateau, rewarded with a visit to the memorial of
Waugh's Well. The walk then follows an old tramway down the valley of
Dearden Clough before skirting the southern slopes of Scout Moor and
crossing the upper reaches of Cheesden Brook, once the site of water-powered mills. It also links with Walk 7 (Top of Leach) giving an opportunity for a
longer walk.

Peaks and Panoramas: KNOWL HILL is a distinctive steep-sided knoll
which dominates the moors north of the Edenfield Road. It has a triangulation
pillar and an excellent viewpoint indicator on its summit and there are views
west, south and east which include Winter Hill, Peel Tower, Manchester,
Rochdale, Blackstone Edge and the Pennines. From here a gently rising
broad plateau leads to the featureless HIGHER HILL and westward to
SCOUT MOOR which reaches its highest point on WHITTLE PIKE, identifiable by its memorial cross. Scout Moor has few other distinctive features
save for the massive building stone quarries cut into its steep western slopes
which dominate the unsightly view from the Irwell Valley below. The panorama from this side of Scout Moor encompasses Rossendale, the Irwell
Valley, Ramsbottom and Holcombe Moor.

Distance: 8 miles

Map: Ordnance Survey Pathfinder 701 Bury, Rochdale and Littleborough

Start: Ashworth Moor Reservoir lay-by, Edenfield Road, near Norden,
Rochdale (Grid Reference 831 159).

Getting there: There is plenty of parking available in this wide lay-by adjacent to the high wall overlooking Ashworth Moor Reservoir and a snack bar is
usually parked up making it a popular spot for passing truckers. The lay-by is
on the moorland route of the A680, roughly halfway between Edenfield and
Rochdale. If travelling from Rochdale, it is on the left of the road just before
Owd Betts Inn is reached on the right. There is also space available in a
rough car park on the right-hand side of the road, which is an old quarry. Alternatively, Owd Betts has a car park if you are imbibing at the hostelry possibly after your expedition.

Public transport: A bus service between Rawtenstall and Rochdale stops at
Ashworth Moor close to Nutter's Restaurant, just a bit further along the road
from Owd Betts and convenient for the start of this walk.

Background

Coal mining, textile mills and stone quarries have tried to destroy the remote upland atmosphere of Scout Moor which forms the western flank of a much broader expanse of Millstone Grit moorland separating Greater Manchester from the towns of the Rossendale Valley. The ridge from Scout Moor east to Top of Leach (see Walk 7) is the highest part of this upland mass geologically referred to as the Rossendale Dome or Anticline. This is an area of rock uplift on the west flank of the main Pennine chain. The Rossendale Dome is cut by the Irwell Valley to the west of Scout Moor and the valley is itself the result of a geological fault, though the moors rise up again beyond it to form the West Pennine Moors from Holcombe over to Winter Hill.

Scout Moor's geology has resulted in the outcropping of layers of sandstone known as Haslingden Flags which lie between bands of weaker shale. The Haslingden Flags are ideal as building stone and this created a mammoth industry in the 19th century as towns grew and new roads and streets were laid out. The great gash on the west side of Scout Moor is testament to this and the flags transported from here have made Rossendale famous. Don't believe anyone who tells you that London's streets are paved with gold, as they are actually paved with Haslingden Flags!

Thin coal seams have also been worked on these moors in the 18th and 19th century and a section of the walk follows an old Coal Road on the south side of the moor, which was used to transport the coal down to the valley below. Just below the Coal Road, the Cheesden Brook rises and this was one of the first industrial rivers in the Manchester region. It flows down to industrial Heywood and joins the River Roch but in the earliest days of the Industrial Revolution its upper reaches near the present line of the Edenfield Road became a site for water-powered textile mills. These employed local handloom weavers and tiny settlements, such as Cheesden Fold, sprung up and enjoyed boom years in the early 19th century before mills no longer relied on fast-flowing water to power their machinery. The ruins of some of the old dwellings are passed near the end of the walk in the pastures below Scout Moor.

All this industrial activity did not stop Edwin Waugh (1817-1890), a son of Rochdale, from finding solace and inspiration in the wilderness of the moor and his writings earned him the reputation of being Lancashire's most renowned dialect poet. His favourite spot was the hillside spring which overlooked the steep valley of Scout Moor Brook

The Wild West of Rossendale

and his followers erected a well here in his honour in 1866. The bust of Edwin Waugh has been added more recently as well as two other memorials, to Ward Ogden and Harry Craven. Waugh's Well is definitely worth a visit and might just inspire you to pen a few lines. The Dialect Society also holds annual pilgrimages to this site.

The busy A680 between Edenfield and Rochdale was turnpiked in the 1790s and the present Owd Betts pub was formerly a roadside inn known as the Hare and Hounds. The New Inn, a bit further along the road towards Edenfield, is now Nutter's Restaurant, an unusual setting for the gastronomic delights provided by celebrity chef, Andrew Nutter.

The Route

1. From the lay-by, take care and cross the road to join the signed public footpath directly opposite into a disused quarry, also used as an informal parking area. There is a wooden sign for Ashworth Moor here and numerous paths, but take one of the obvious tracks forking off right up the side of the quarry and Knowl Hill will quickly be seen in the distance. Bear right and take the wide, well-used track which heads directly for the hill and soon reaches a gate and stile. Cross this and continue along the track that leads steeply up the left-hand side of Knowl Hill, distinctively flat-topped with steep sides. A triangulation pillar and viewpoint indicator erected by the Naden Valley Conservation Group are found on top and if conditions are perfect you may see such sights as Jodrell Bank (48km away) and the Welsh Mountains (128km away). Closer at hand are the Peel Tower, Ashworth Reservoir, Norden and Rochdale.

2. From the indicator, drop steeply down the back of Knowl Hill and pick out the distinctive boggy path which heads north across the open moor keeping to the right and slightly above the even boggier line of a wide drainage ditch. Though this is not a definitive right of way, it is well-used by walkers and the tracks of mountain bikes have also managed to work their way through the quagmire. The straight boggy line is followed for almost a mile and heads towards a line of hills on the horizon which includes Whittle Hill, on the left-hand side of the ridge, with a small cross on top of it. The path peters out slightly as you near the ridge but simply head for the wall facing you and pick out a stile in the boundary fence. The higher ground on the far side of the stile is Higher Hill, but there is nothing

of interest there so do not cross the stile. Instead, turn right and follow the wall-side along a distinct path across the upper reaches of the Naden Brook, with the Naden Valley almost hidden from view down to the right. Keep to the wall-side and, when it changes direction, turning sharp left, turn sharp left with it and follow it around to where it meets two stone gateposts on either side of a grassy track.

3. Do not go through the gateway, but turn right and follow the grassy track slightly downhill as it runs between a wall and the steep sided valley of a little brook. The brook is crossed and meanders its way down an interesting steep-sided chasm that looks like something out of the Wild West. Continue along the track that climbs along the opposite side of the valley and, when a wall is reached, the track forks. Follow the lower path which shortly leads you to Waugh's Well, on the right. This was erected in 1866 and has other memorials in its stonework – it's a pleasant spot to rest and watch the gulls on the reservoir below. Across the valley, Whittle Hill rises to a summit cross. Faint paths lead up it from all directions and there is a steep ascent from the reservoir below if you wish to explore the summit, Whittle Pike. On the summit, there is a cross in memory of Flying Officer Geoffrey Molyneux, lost in operations in 1955 and the founder of a Bury scout group. The cross was erected by his troop in 1983.

4. To resume the walk from Waugh's Well, continue along the path and you soon pass the ruins of an old farm on the right. Shortly after this, the wall on the left of the path changes direction and, at this point, turn left and drop down the hill to join a reservoir access road. The definitive right of way is difficult to spot on the ground but the route aims to cross Scout Moor Brook, which flows out of the small reservoir below, and then to climb up to the opposite side of the valley. The easiest way to do this is to follow the reservoir access road downhill for a short distance until it meanders sharply around the hill. As you come around the corner of the hill, turn right off the track and drop steeply down to the brook along the straight line of a semi-derelict wall to the immediate left. Keep to the wall-side and cross the brook, climbing diagonally right up the steep valley side opposite to join a faint grass track almost hidden in rushes close to two wooden posts in a gateway.

5. Turn right along this track which becomes more distinct as it proceeds down the valley, whilst maintaining its height above the

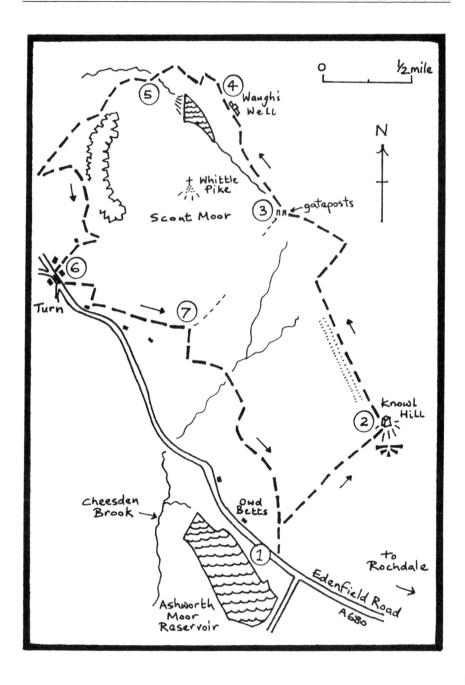

brook, down to the right. Scout Moor Brook joins Dearden Brook in the valley below and the track heads in the same general direction and follows the line of an old quarry tramway with wooden sleepers (slippery when wet) and iron rails still in evidence. The tramway is followed for over a mile and becomes a grassy track running below quarry workings and rock heaps. It bears left around the hillside above the wooded Dearden Clough and aims directly towards the Peel Tower on the far side of the Irwell Valley. Eventually, a wall with two gates is reached beyond a thick patch of rushes. Do not go through the kissing gate facing you but turn sharp left and head up the side of the wall, keeping it to the right. At the top of the field, the wall bends around to the right and a grass track is joined. Turn right and the track soon meets a tarmac quarry access road. Go directly across this and continue straight ahead along the hillside, keeping close to a wall on the right and aiming directly for the mill chimney in Turn village. Drop down the hill slightly to cross a brook and turn right to cross a stile by a white cottage. Turn left and follow the drive-way past cottages to reach the 'A' road.

6. You are now in the tiny village of Turn. Take a left turn, cross over and follow the pavement for a very short distance past houses until Lodge Mill Lane is reached on the right. A stile in the wall will be seen on the left here, so cross back over and join this path which leads directly and steeply uphill to another stile at the top of the field. Cross this and turn right along an overgrown track which leads downhill towards a cottage. Turn left at the fence boundary and fol-low the fence side on a grassy path that runs parallel to the road just below it. Keep to this grassy track (known as the Coal Road), above the road and below the steep slopes of Scout Moor, for about half a mile until a ladder stile is reached in the corner of a wall on the right of the track.

7. Cross this stile and head straight downhill alongside the wall bound-ary to reach another stile. Do not go over this stile, instead turn left in the same field and follow the fence and then a wall-side to cross an-other stile and drop down steps to a footbridge over the Cheesden Brook. Climb the steps on the far side of the brook and bear right, keeping a wall to the right. When the wall ends, keep going in the same direction, aiming for the walled remains of an old farmhouse. Pass the ruins and join another path, running left to right. Bear right up the hillside to reach a wall gap on a little spur known as Tom Hill.

Go through the open gateway and continue in the same direction, with the wall to the left. The grassy path provides a pleasant view to Ashworth Moor Reservoir and Owd Betts and soon crosses a ladder stile in a wall. Cross this and the path bears right across pastures and heads directly towards the reservoir and soon meets the Edenfield Road at the point where the walk was started.

7. Top of Leach

This walk traverses a moorland horseshoe above the Naden Valley, beginning with a steep climb up Knowl Hill then a long boggy hike bearing north and east to the summit of Top of Leach, virtually the highest point in the Borough of Rossendale. From here, there is an easy and gradual descent along the paved Rooley Moor Road to Greenbooth Reservoir and the industrial hamlet of Wolstenholme. The walk then heads back to the Edenfield Road through fields and along the lane passing the hidden farms of Ashworth Moor from where there are excellent views across the city and the Pennines. Note that this walk is strenuous, due to a few miles of bog-trotting across open moorland with no discernible track. There should be no navigation problems in clear conditions but the relevant O.S. Pathfinder map will certainly be required. It also links with Walk 6 (Scout Moor) giving an opportunity for a longer walk.

Peaks and Panoramas: KNOWL HILL is a distinctive steep-sided plateau overlooking the Edenfield Road which has a triangulation pillar and viewpoint indicator on its summit. It is also visited in Walk 6. HAIL STORM HILL and TOP OF LEACH form a broad plateau at the head of the Naden Valley and the slopes on their north and south sides have been much affected by quarrying. TOP OF LEACH is only easy to pick out because it has a tall stone plinth engraved with the townships that make up Rossendale and is topped by a viewpoint indicator. It also has a small stone shelter and triangulation pillar. The summit lies just within the boundary of Rossendale Borough. ROOLEY MOOR is the long moorland spur on the east side of the Naden Valley which runs south to form a little peak at TOP OF PIKE and is crossed by an old paved road. The views from Knowl Hill and Rooley Moor mainly look southwards to Rochdale, the city and the Pennines. But Top of the Leach provides an outlook northwards as well, to Rossendale, Pendle Hill, Penyghent and Ingleborough.

Distance: 10 miles

Map: Ordnance Survey Pathfinder 701 Bury, Rochdale and Littleborough

Start: Ashworth Moor Reservoir lay-by, Edenfield Road, near Norden, Rochdale (Grid Reference 831 159).

Getting there: There is plenty of parking available in this wide lay-by adjacent to the high wall overlooking Ashworth Moor Reservoir and a snack bar is usually parked up making it a popular spot for passing truckers. The lay-by is on the moorland route of the A680, roughly halfway between Edenfield and Rochdale. If travelling from Rochdale, it is on the left of the road just before Owd Betts Inn is reached on the right. There is also space available in a rough car park on the right-hand side of the road, which is an old quarry. Alternatively, Owd Betts has a car park if you are imbibing at the hostelry possibly after your expedition.

Public transport: A bus service between Rawtenstall and Rochdale stops at Ashworth Moor close to Nutter's Restaurant which is just a bit further along the road from Owd Betts and is convenient for the start of this walk.

Background

This walk is very much a contrast to many of the well waymarked routes to be found elsewhere in this book. The high moors between Rochdale and Rossendale have a rights of way network on the map which bears little relation to routes walked on the ground and the definitive routes are very much a legacy of an age before such paths were used largely for recreation. The good waymarking fairy also seems to have given this area a miss. Do not despair though, for the section of this walk over the bleak Rossendale moors is easy enough in good weather and with a constant view of the city centre to guide the way you are not so far from civilisation as you might think.

The boggy stretch of moorland between Knowl Hill and Top of Leach is a desolate trudge across the higher part of the geological uplift known as the Rossendale Dome which has already been described in Walk 6. The county boundary between Greater Manchester and Rossendale, which has only existed since 1974, runs along the ridge of Hail Storm Hill and Top of Leach. The hexagonal summit stone records the five former townships which make up the new Rossendale Borough: Whitworth, Bacup, Rawtenstall, Haslingden and part of Ramsbottom. Top of Leach has a hard cap of rock and surprisingly it is slightly higher than Blackstone Edge on the main Pennine chain. However, below its summit, as with Scout Moor to the west, its slopes have been quarried for the layers of Haslingden Flags. Amaze your friends with the fascinating fact that the Top of Leach trig. point is the highest in Rossendale!

The Rooley Moor Road is an old packhorse route that ran from Rochdale to Rossendale though its paving was not undertaken until the 1860s during a time when the Cotton Famine, resulting from the American Civil War, affected the Lancashire the cotton industry. Unemployed textile workers were used to improve the road. Note also that, in the 1930s Depression, unemployed textile workers constructed Watergrove Reservoir (see Walk 8). The Ashworth Moor Reservoir, alongside the turnpike road from Edenfield to Rochdale, is an Edwar-

The Naden Valley

dian construction of the Heywood and Middleton Water Board and was completed in 1908.

The Rossendale Way, often seen waymarked with an 'R.W.', is a 45 mile route which takes in the moorlands on both sides of the Rossendale Valley. It was officially opened in 1985 and the event is marked by a memorial stone on Rooley Moor Road below Top of Leach.

The reservoirs of the Naden Valley were constructed in the 19th century initially to supply water to numerous bleachworks situated along the Naden Brook. The reservoirs are almost hidden due to the steep-sided profile of the valley, the result of a geological fault cutting deep into the Rossendale uplift.

The Route

1. The first few miles of this walk are the same as for the start of Walk 6. From the lay-by, join the signed public footpath on the opposite side of the road into a disused quarry, now used as a car park. There is a wooden sign for Ashworth Moor here and numerous paths; take one of the obvious tracks forking off right up the side of the quarry and

Knowl Hill will quickly be seen in the distance. Bear right and take the wide well-used track which heads directly for the hill and soon reaches a gate and stile. Cross this and continue along the track which leads steeply up the left-hand side of Knowl Hill, distinctively flat-topped with steep sides. A triangulation pillar and viewpoint indicator erected by the Naden Valley Conservation Group are found on top and there are good views southwards including to nearby Peel Tower, Ashworth Reservoir, Norden and Rochdale.

2. From the indicator, drop steeply down the back of Knowl Hill and a vast expanse of bleak moorland lies before you. Pick out the distinctive boggy path which heads north across the open moor, keeping to the right and slightly above the even boggier line of a wide drainage ditch. Though this is not a definitive right of way, it is well-used by walkers and the tracks of mountain bikes have also managed to work their way through the quagmire. The straight, boggy path is followed for almost a mile and heads towards a line of hills on the horizon; this includes Whittle Hill, on the left-hand side of the ridge, which has a small cross on top of it. The path peters out slightly as you near the ridge but simply head for the wall facing you and pick out a stile in the boundary fence. The higher ground on the far side of the stile is Higher Hill, but there is nothing of interest there, so do not cross the stile. Instead, turn right and follow the wall-side along a distinct path which crosses the upper reaches of the Naden Brook with the Naden Valley, almost hidden from view down to the right. Shortly, the corner of the wall/fence is reached and it changes direction by a stile on the left.

3. Do not turn left with the wall here (unlike the previous walk). Instead, the route heads across the open moor (not a definitive right of way), without any visible path on the ground, to reach the summit of Top of Leach. The summit cannot be seen from the wall corner but just continue straight ahead in the same general direction as you have been walking – do not drop down to the slopes on your right. If anything, bear slightly left and keep to the higher ground across the plateau appropriately marked on the map as Hail Storm Hill. Watch your footing, as several wet springs are crossed. The trudge across can seem quite pleasant if you look back to your right for a view of the city centre beyond Knowl Hill – surely Hail Storm Hill is better than shopping in the Arndale Centre! Pass over the brow of Hail Storm Hill and, at last, visible features appear on the moor ahead. A

collection of stones can be seen nearby and, behind them, a stone structure – the plinth on Top of Leach. Head for the stones, parts of old quarry workings, and cross a waymarked track here (a public bridleway). Continue straight ahead directly towards the stone structures (three of them) and you may be able to pick out a faint path leading to them. Look left (northwards) and the Rossendale Hills and, hopefully, Pendle Hill and the Yorkshire Peaks can be seen. Shortly, the viewpoint indicator is reached on Top of Leach summit.

4. The hexagonal stone from a local quarry is engraved with the names of the five townships of Rossendale. With the aid of the viewpointer, you may be able to pick out Ingleborough (the one to the left) and Penyghent, Pendle Hill, Blackstone Edge, the Peak District, Bury, Rochdale and Manchester, fifteen miles away. There is also a triangulation pillar and wall shelter on the summit. Continue in the same direction from the summit and the massive quarry above Whitworth comes into view. Drop down to a paved track, the Rooley Moor Road. Up on the left, alongside the track, is a memorial that is easily missed – a stone wall commemorating the opening of the Rossendale Way in 1985. Turn right along the paved route, followed for the next 2 miles generally downhill with a view left to the Watergrove hills (see Walk 8) and right to the reservoirs of the Naden Valley. The paved road becomes cobbled and runs past the ruins of an inn and below the cairned hill known as Top of Pike. It then runs straight downhill as a stony track towards pylons and with a view of the seven tower blocks of Rochdale town centre straight ahead. Hollingworth Lake and the M62 viaduct behind it are also clearly seen. As the pylons are approached, look out for a wooden waymarker signpost on the right of the track.

5. Leave Rooley Moor Road here by turning right and following the track signed for Greenbooth. The track swings around the hill and drops down to a tarmac lane. Continue straight ahead here towards the reservoirs. Keep to the lane as it turns sharp left and crosses a cattle grid. Follow it downhill for approximately a quarter of a mile, passing the entrances to Brownhill Farm and Sidholme Farm. After passing the second farm, look for a stile, gate, footpath signpost and North West Water sign on the right. Cross the stile and follow the field-edge path under the pylons to another stile and gate. The path soon forks by an open gateway above the reservoir. Turn left here

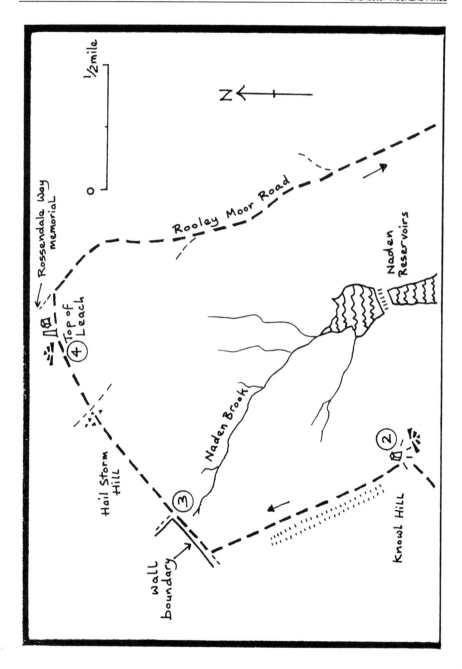

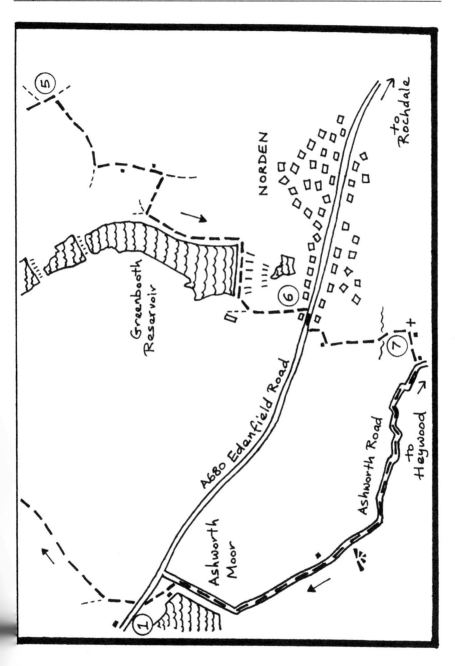

and join the path leading along the bank of Greenbooth Reservoir, which passes a memorial bench and runs above conifers with the reservoir to the right. The well-maintained path leads all the way to a gate and turning circle at the end of the reservoir dam. Cross the high dam and note the tablet in the wall which commemorates the village of Greenbooth, submerged under the reservoir. Follow the main reservoir track as it swings left beyond the dam to reach blue Water Authority gates that lead out onto a lane. Turn left here and follow the lane down to where it joins the A680 Edenfield Road by the White Lion pub.

6. Turn right and follow the road through Wolstenholme for approximately 150 metres. Then cross over and join a track which runs off the road to the right of a row of cottages. The track is not waymarked, but a plaque on the last cottage notes it as the access to Laneside Farm. The track runs past the cottages, then swings right and passes by the front of the farm. Immediately after the farm, swing left and follow a grass path which crosses a step in a wall and runs along a field edge with a wooded valley on the right. Some waymarkers would be useful here but, as the path drops downhill, turn right and cross the brook by a very muddy ford. Swing left on the far side of the brook and climb up the muddy bank to follow the field edge, with the woodland on the left. In the corner of the field, cross a stile hidden behind a holly bush and join a track. Bear left but, almost straight ahead, on the opposite side of the track, join a narrow path between holly bushes. The pleasant hedged path leads down stone steps to a footbridge. Cross this and bear right to climb up wooden steps to a bank of heather and another stile. There is a good view back to the moors just walked from here. Cross the stile and follow the field edge up to Ashworth Moor's church and pub, the Egerton Arms, hidden in the back of beyond.

7. Turn right on the track leading to the church and pub and follow it back to a road. A sign on the corner states that the Egerton Arms is over 500 years old. Turn right on Ashworth Moor Road and follow this meandering lane for two miles all the way to Ashworth Moor Reservoir. The road is mainly used by farm traffic and is a better alternative to the busier Edenfield Road and also some dodgy, unwaymarked rights of way that pass through farmyards with barking dogs further north. The Ashworth Moor Road also gives exceptionally good views both to the north and south – and particularly to the Pennines and the city centre. The road twists and turns a lot so be wary of traffic, particularly on Sundays when all the bikers and charabancs come out. After nearly three-quarters of a mile, the road starts to climb to Wind Hill and from here the view starts to open out to the flat plain of the city and Heaton Park Tower can be seen. As the road climbs, do not go too close to Wind Hill Farm (on the right) as there are several angry-looking dogs that will bark and growl – but are thankfully chained up. The road drops to the reservoir beyond Wind Hill and passes it on the right. Turn left after passing the gates of the 1908 house overlooking the reservoir and follow the wide verge of Edenfield Road back to the lay-by.

8. Rough Hill

This walk is a perfect valley horseshoe, traversing the arc of hills that encloses the catchment brooks of the Watergrove Reservoir above Wardle village. It climbs several distinctive knolls to reach its highest point on Rough Hill at the head of the valley before crossing the old packhorse route of the Long Causeway and returning to the reservoir shore. There is no road walking at all on this route except along the reservoir access road. From the dam of Watergrove Reservoir, you can see the whole route laid out before you.

Peaks and Panoramas: BROWN WARDLE HILL, MIDDLE HILL, HADES HILL, ROUGH HILL and CROOK HILL form the triangle of moorland mounds which enclose the Watergrove Valley. Brown Wardle Hill and Middle Hill, on the west of the valley, are distinctive as they are perfectly shaped hills – conical with steep sides – but Middle Hill has been much affected by quarrying. Brown Wardle Hill used to have a triangulation pillar but this has been destroyed and now there is a just a summit cairn. Hades Hill and Rough Hill are at the top of the valley and link to form a fairly featureless plateau with nothing of interest save the views. Crook Hill is also a broad area of moorland though on top of it stands a circular wall shelter. All these hills share a wide panorama south to Wardle, Rochdale, Littleborough and Greater Manchester. Brown Wardle and Middle Hills offer views west to Whitworth and Rossendale and Crook Hill looks east to the Pennines with Blackstone Edge and Windy Hill very easy to spot. Rough Hill also looks north to Rossendale, the Calder Valley and the peaks of the Yorkshire Dales.

Distance: 8 miles

Map: Ordnance Survey Outdoor Leisure Sheet 21, South Pennines or Pathfinder Sheet 701 Bury, Rochdale and Littleborough

Start: Watergrove Reservoir (Trap Farm) car park, Wardle Fold, Wardle, near Rochdale (Grid Reference 912 176).

Getting there: There are only two roads leading into Wardle and both lead off from the A58 between Rochdale and Littleborough. If approaching from Rochdale, the road to Wardle is signed and leaves the A58 between two pubs, the Bull's Head and Sandknockers. To reach the reservoir car park, drive all the way through the village until you can go no further. The road ends at Watergrove Reservoir and a cobbled road (not good for your car's suspension) leads through blue gates to the large car park below the dam.

Public transport: Bus services stop at the northern end of the village, at the Chapel terminus in the village square where there is a turning area for buses. Services from Rochdale to Wardle (via Birch Hill Hospital) and from Rochdale to Littleborough both stop here. It is then a short walk up Ramsden Road to join the cobbled lane leading to the reservoir.

Background

The cobbled road that leads up to the dam of Watergrove Reservoir once continued up the valley and linked with a pack horse route that traversed the moors and dropped down into Yorkshire's Calder Valley at Todmorden. This was, of course, before the reservoir was built in the 1930s and Ramsden Road was the village street of an old settlement called Watergrove which rests below the waters of its artificially created namesake.

Watergrove Reservoir

From the 17th century to the 1900s, Watergrove was a bustling rural community that survived in an impoverished area. The village folk were sheep farmers, colliers, hand-loom weavers and quarrymen – often having to tackle two or more jobs. The ruined farmsteads, abandoned quarries and mine spoil heaps are a legacy of this past age and in the reservoir wall (passed at the end of this walk) numerous village datestones have been preserved, proving that there once was life here. Many of the old farms had 17th century datestones and an 1881 plaque from Watergrove Mill has been set in the wall, one of several mills that were built in the valley. Watergrove Mill stood along the northern edge of the present reservoir whilst Alderbank Mill is beneath it, along with the village pubs and Methodist church.

Before the 19th century mills came, the hardy farmers dug out coal from shallow pits in the hillside or sold their wool to the wool 'broggers', the tradesmen who became a familiar site on these moors even in the 16th and 17th centuries. The 'broggers' took the wool on packhorses to the great markets in Rochdale and Halifax where it was sold to cloth merchants. It was between these two towns that the main artery of the cross-Pennine wool trade flowed. Packhorse routes radiated out from the towns, meandering over moors and through the valleys which linked Lancashire and Yorkshire. The Blackstone Edge road is one such example (See Walk 9) as is the Long Causeway, passed on this walk. Largely paved with stone flags, to provide a hard surface for horses crossing steep and usually boggy slopes, this route crossed over to the Calder Valley from Rochdale and probably linked with the ancient route of the same name, which ran from Burnley to Halifax via Hebden Bridge.

It was the decline in the textile industry that eventually ended Watergrove's halcyon days. In the 1930s, the village disappeared like Atlantis beneath the shimmering waters of a reservoir that had taken unemployed mill workers eight years to dig. It's all history now, together with the ruined farmsteads which were abandoned to preserve the water quality. Thankfully, Watergrove is an excellent advertisement for North West Water, who are fulfilling their duty to provide for recreation quite admirably. There is a network of walking trails around the valley, fishing, windsurfing, a wildlife reserve and a ranger station with information panels which outline the history of Watergrove.

The Route

1. From the car park, climb the wooden staircase up the reservoir dam. Looking north beyond the reservoir, the moorland horseshoe to be traversed can be seen with Rough Hill at the head of the valley. Turn left and follow the path along the dam to the corner of the reservoir. Continue straight ahead at the end of the reservoir along a green track that heads towards a fence on a hill. Just below the fence, a track from Wardle village is joined at a bridle gate with blue and yellow waymarkers. Go straight ahead through the bridle gate and, almost immediately, a wall is reached. Veer left around the wall, then turn sharp right, following the track along the far side of it. With the wall and ditch on the right, follow the track uphill as it bears left towards a group of trees. The trees are passed on the right and a post with a yellow and green South Pennine Chain waymarker. Go through an old gateway and bear right along a track to another bridle gate. Go through this and turn left to follow a stone track towards a white house on the hill (actually, a golf clubhouse). Follow the meandering track towards the moorland golf course for about a third of a mile until an obvious crossroads of paths and tracks is reached.

2. Bear right along a track here to reach a wooden signpost waymarked with 'R.W.' (Rossendale Way). Two tracks fork off here, take the left one which follows the higher ground and follows a grass path uphill towards the conical-shaped Brown Wardle Hill. Over to the left there is a view towards Whitworth, beyond which rises Rooley Moor. The path rises steeply up the south side of Brown Wardle Hill ands leads directly to the summit. The triangulation pillar marked on the map has gone but there is a cairn. The far-reaching views from here towards the Pennines, Rochdale, Oldham and the city centre are maintained for the rest of this moorland traverse. Hollingworth Lake, the M62 Rakewood viaduct, Blackstone Edge and Windy Hill mast are all easily identified. Drop steeply down the north side of the hill with views left to the Rossendale Valley. Cross a track running left to right and follow the obvious path which leads steeply up the right of Middle Hill, passing further R.W. waymarkers. Keep to the grassy path below the summit of Middle Hill and pass below a collection of quarry heaps. When the path appears to peter out in a patch of boggy rushes, bear left and head uphill to the higher ground where a yellow-painted stone waymarker marked with an 'H' is reached.

3. The stone waymarker is easily missed as it hidden in rushes but it is just below a Rossendale Way signpost and blue waymarker post at a junction of tracks. Turn right at the waymarker stone, follow a sunken grass track which heads uphill, and keep a semi-derelict wall on your right. It passes a walled ruin on the right and, when the wall completely disappears, follow the path along the edge of a fairly flat-topped plateau. The highest points of Hades Hill and Rough Hill lie to the left but, for the moment, keep to the right of way – a bridleway, which runs along the head of the valley and offers a fine view down to the ruined farmhouses above Watergrove Reservoir. Eventually, two waymarker posts are reached at a junction of paths.

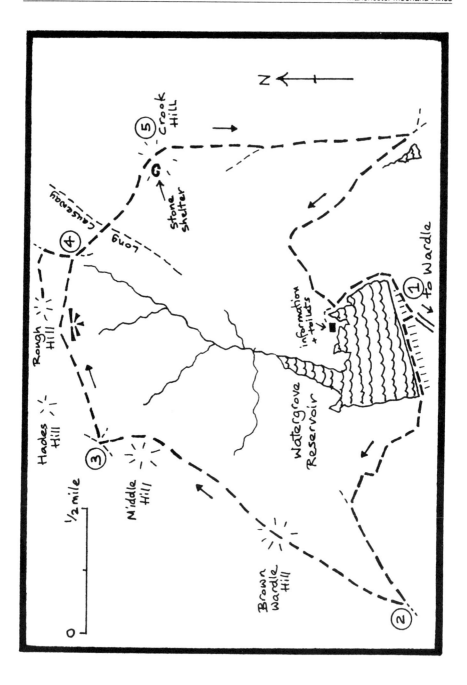

It is worth diverting from here to climb the summit of Rough Hill just to obtain the views – so, at the first post, turn left and follow the bridleway up the valley for about a quarter of a mile then turn sharp left and take a faint path leading uphill to the summit. There is a small cairn on the boggy plateau but nothing else save the good views north to the Calder Valley, Cliviger wind farms, Pendle Hill and, hopefully, the Yorkshire Dales. Also east to the Stoodley Pike monument. From here, retrace your steps down to the waymarker post.

4. At the second waymarker post, take the path forking left. This is a public footpath, which follows the higher ground and climbs gradually to reach another crossroads of routes. The track running left to right down the hill is the Long Causeway, the old packhorse route which is stone paved in places. This walk only crosses it but, if you follow it down the hillside for a very short distance, you will be able to see it heading directly for the reservoir – though it once ran all the way to Watergrove village. However, continue straight ahead at the crossroads and follow the path which climbs gradually over Crook Moor. After nearly half a mile, a well-built circular stone shelter is reached on Crook Hill. This forms the western end of another broad flat-topped plateau, which runs east to Shore Moor and drops steeply to the Summit Road between Littleborough and Todmorden. There are good views over to the Pennines from here – you can even see the White House pub on the A58 to the left of Blackstone Edge. Rochdale and Oldham town centres are also easy to identify – Rochdale has a row of seven tower blocks (next to Hopwood Hall College on the A58), Oldham has one high-rise block on a hill.

5. Continue downhill from the stone shelter along a grassy track that passes a pond on the left. The path heads directly south along the hill spur for nearly three quarters of a mile and passes under pylons to reach a gate in a wall alongside a ruined enclosure. Do not go through the gate but turn sharp right before it and follow the track which leads back under the pylons and climbs gradually uphill alongside a wall. Two ladder stiles are passed on the left and eventually a waymarked gate is reached in the wall on the left. Go through this and follow a cobbled track around the hillside which drops downhill towards the reservoir. Go through another gate and down to the reservoir access road. Go through the kissing gate opposite to join a path along the reservoir shore, which avoids the road. Turn

right if you want to reach the information point, but turn left to continue the walk and follow the path back towards the dam. A kissing gate leads back onto the road at the corner of the reservoir and in the wall to your right look out for the numerous datestones preserved from Watergrove village. Follow the access road, which swings right and goes through a gate to reach the car park. You are back in dog-walking country.

9. Blackstone Edge

This walk climbs an ancient moorland road up to the high Pennines, joining the Pennine Way footpath to traverse Blackstone Edge and Windy Hill, crossing the M62 before descending to pastures around Hollingworth Lake. It links with Walk 10 (White Hill) giving opportunities for a longer walk.

Peaks and Panoramas: BLACKSTONE EDGE and WINDY HILL are traversed along the Pennine Way and both are easily identifiable. Blackstone Edge has a long line of distinctive gritstone crags and hidden among them is a summit triangulation pillar. Windy Hill lies just the other side of the M62 motorway and has a stout radio mast, which makes it easy to pick out from miles around. From these Pennine tops, there are views south and west to Rochdale, Oldham, Manchester and the hills around Saddleworth. Looking north there are views to the Rossendale moors including the wind farm at Cliviger. The route is also on the edge of Yorkshire here and there are extensive views east to the moors above Calderdale, including a sighting of the Stoodley Pike monument.

Distance: 9½ miles

Map: Ordnance Survey Pathfinder 701 Bury, Rochdale and Littleborough

Start: Hollingworth Lake Country Park car park, Rakewood Road, Littleborough (Grid Reference 939 153).

Getting there: Hollingworth Lake Country Park is reached via the B6225 road that runs between Littleborough and Milnrow. At the Fisherman's Inn turn off on to Rakewood Road, the lane that skirts around the lake. The entrance to the Country Park is signed approximately 150 metres further up the lane from the Inn. The car park is Pay and Display – allow at least 4 hours for this walk.

Public transport: Bus services from Rochdale to Hollingworth Lake, some of which continue to Littleborough, stop at the Fisherman's Inn, very close to the start of the walk. Alternatively, there is a train station at Littleborough on the line from Manchester to Rochdale, Halifax and Leeds. From the station head south along Hollingworth Road which brings you straight to the shore of Hollingworth Lake. The return journey from Littleborough station to the start of the walk will add approximately 1¼ miles to the walk route.

Background

I always wanted my ashes scattered over Blackstone Edge so that I could spend eternity looking down on Lancashire. This needs to be done on a calm day, otherwise a sudden gust of wind might blow me into Yorkshire. It is a fine place to observe the quintessential northern landscape of textile towns overlooked by bleak moors, though tower blocks are now a more common sight than mill chimneys in the view across Rochdale, Oldham and Bury.

Hollingworth Lake is a reminder of the old days when the lake shore resembled a mini-Blackpool and Victorians would disembark here to enjoy promenading, novelty amusements, boating, skating and steamers across the Lake to the Lake Hotel. The Lake was actually created as a feeder lodge to maintain the water level in the Rochdale Canal (built 1794-1802). Captain Webb trained here before he became the first man to swim the English Channel in 1875 and he returned here again to compete in races. Visitors still flock here for ice creams and pub lunches, the Lake is calm and serene against the menacing backdrop of Blackstone Edge and the M62 Rakewood viaduct.

The climb from the lake leads to the row of cottages that make up the tiny hamlet of Lydgate, which once stood on the old turnpike road from Rochdale and Littleborough over the moors to Halifax. There even use to be a pub here called the Gate Inn, known for its egg-judging competitions (no doubt popular before karaoke nights). The new turnpike route, the present A58, follows a more gradual climb out of Littleborough and was already in use in the 19th century when mail coaches to York were thundering over the moor.

A much older road, once known as the Dhoul's Pavement, climbs steeply from Lydgate to the Blackstone Edge ridge and has been the subject of much debate for centuries. It is known that Roman armies built a line of communication across the Pennines to link the fort at Manchester (Mamucium) to the old Brigantian capital at Aldborough (Isurium), which lies close to the modern A1 near Boroughbridge. The wide, stone-flagged road at Blackstone Edge is reputed to be a preserved section of this ancient route and the finest surviving example of a Roman road in the country. Or was it medieval in origin? It was certainly used as a packhorse route and was an important route for wool 'broggers' involved in the Lancashire and Yorkshire textile trade. The Aiggin Stone is also marked on maps and is an old road boundary stone, which has also been the subject of similar debate – Roman or medieval? In both cases – you decide!

The famous traveller Daniel Defoe climbed up to Blackstone Edge on his grand tour in the 1720s and panicked in a snow storm. He was, of course, a southern softie but quaintly described the Pennines as the 'Andes of the North'. He also described the ridge as a 'fearful precipice'

Blackstone Edge summit

which it can appear, particularly if you peer over the edge of one of the towering gritstone buttresses which shape the summit. On Ordnance Survey maps, the summit hereabouts is often referred to as Robin Hood's Bed. I don't think he slept here, but this is another example of the legendary hero's name being associated with geographical features across the north. From graves, to bays to rocks, Robin pops up all over the place like a sort of medieval Ronald McDonald.

The M62 is neither Roman, medieval or Victorian, but circa late 1960s. Its gradient could only be maintained by such huge engineering feats as building the Rakewood viaduct over the valley of Longden End Brook and the deep cutting underneath the Pennine Way footbridge. The Pennine Way (see also Walk 10) was the inspiration of the late great Tom Stephenson and was officially opened in 1965. Thankfully, its route was retained after the motorway was cut without any tiresome diversion (see also Walk 10).

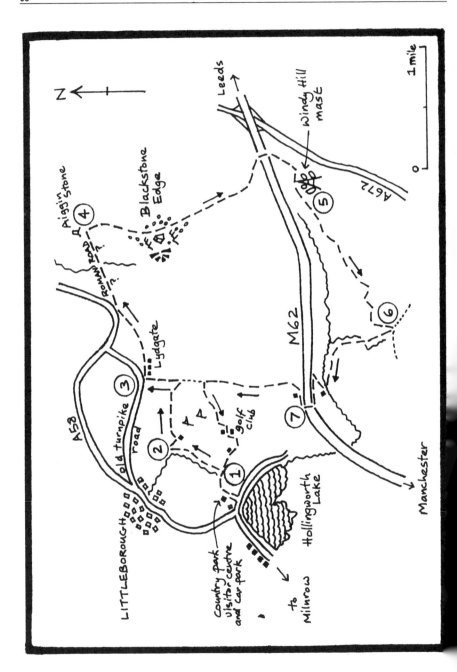

The Route

1. From the rear of the visitor centre car park follow the narrow tarmac access road that runs in a straight line between trees and passes through a metal gate. The road soon swings right and passes a picnic area to reach a field gate. Go through the gate, cross the brook and immediately turn sharp left, following the field edge to cross another footbridge. Keeping the woodland and the brook on your left, go through kissing gates to join a stone path with a view of the Blackstone Edge crags rising dramatically skywards on your right. The stone path soon reaches an access road alongside a footpath signpost.

2. Turn left on the access road and follow it for approximately 130 metres until a footpath is reached on your right. Take this path, which climbs steeply uphill to a woodland behind a house. At the top of the hill, turn left and follow the distinct path at the edge of the woodland above the brook until a culvert is reached by a waymarked kissing gate. Go through the gate to enter Whittaker golf course. Beware of golf balls here! Follow the path uphill between greens and it soon becomes a distinct track. Follow this track as it gradually climbs straight in the direction of the high hills. Pass through a kissing gate and the track swings left to reach a lane. Turn left along the lane and walk slightly downhill for about a quarter of a mile to reach a roadside cluster of cottages – the tiny hamlet of Lydgate.

3. Turn right and follow the track uphill between the pleasant row of cottages and their gardens. Go through the gate beyond the cottages and follow the grassy path uphill with a stone wall on your right. Follow this path for about half a mile as it climbs uphill and swings left almost to join the A58 Rochdale-Halifax road. Close to the road, the path continues as a distinct track running directly up the hillside to the left of the dark crags of Blackstone Edge. Follow the track uphill, this is the supposed Roman road from Manchester to Aldborough, which was certainly used as a medieval packhorse route. The cobbles of the old road are nicely exposed in places, particularly after a drain is crossed – from which point you are walking along the Pennine Way long-distance footpath. Near the top of the ridge a stone pillar is reached on your left – this is the Aiggin Stone and is not particularly exciting despite its possible antiquity.

4. On the opposite side of the packhorse road to the Aiggin Stone is a kissing gate. Go through this and follow the path across the open moor up to the rock buttresses on the summit of Blackstone Edge. The path to the crags and the summit trig point is fairly distinct as it meanders between gritstone boulders and there are waymarker posts to guide you, particularly in bad weather. There are breathtaking views from the summit in all directions, from Manchester city centre over to Yorkshire in the east. To the north can be seen the Stoodley Pike monument (to the Napoleonic Wars) and a number of Pennine wind farms. The distinctive West Pennine landmarks of Winter Hill, Holcombe Moor and Knowl Hill can also be seen on clear days. From the triangulation pillar rejoin the Pennine Way path which heads southwards like a ribbon in the direction of a tall radio mast on Windy Hill. There is now a long trudge towards the mast, heading gradually downhill for about one and a quarter miles to reach a dramatic high footbridge over the noisy M62. Cross here and don't let your hat (or wig) blow off as you will never retrieve it. Climb directly up to the mast on the opposite side of the motorway. On reaching the access road to the mast, say goodbye to the Pennine Way and turn right up the road.

5. The path quickly forks right, passing the transmitter station on your left and behind the transmitter the path forks again. Take the right fork and follow the bridleway, which drops downhill to an open gateway in a derelict wall. This spur is marked as Windy Hill on the Ordnance Survey map and gives its name to the wireless station just passed. The path forks again, keep to the left fork, keeping to the left of the hill spur with a wall immediately to your right. Follow this path alongside the wall as it follows the top of a prominent ridge which overlooks the reservoirs of the Piethorn Valley far below to your left. A good view of Manchester is soon revealed. After about three-quarters of a mile, the path becomes a green lane between walls, follow this and it eventually swings sharp left around the hillside to a crossroads of paths with a variety of waymarkers.

6. Turn sharp right where the paths meet and almost immediately turn right to climb over the metal ladder stile in the wall, indicated by a blue waymarker. Go directly across the small enclosure, crossing a derelict wall and pick up the faint path which leads through rough pasture and heads down the valley. Keep the boggy area and wall to your left. The wall ends and then the path crosses over to the opposite side of the boggy area, which marks the upper end of a steep-sided little valley. Continue in the direction of the motorway, skirting the hillside above the valley, now to your right. The path then drops quite steeply down the hillside and joins a track in the valley bottom. Join this track, bearing left, which leads downhill to trees and a cottage below the motorway. Cross the footbridge and follow the path which leads through a gate to the right of the cottage. This swings right and leads steeply uphill, then turning left and going through a gate to join an access track running alongside the motorway. When the road bridge over the M62 is reached, turn right and cross the motorway.

7. On the far side of the motorway turn right, pass the cottage and go through the gate to join a track that heads directly north across the moor. Follow this for about a mile until you meet Whittaker Lane on your left, the road which comes up from the golf club which can be seen below. Turn down this lane which drops downhill to the clubhouse. Continue straight ahead at the clubhouse buildings and a footpath then swings right and heads diagonally through a woodland. At the edge of the woodland there is a junction of paths. Take the right fork and the path leads downhill to cross a stream and then turn right, passing a farm building on your right. A farm track leads downhill and leads back to the gate into the picnic area of the country park. Follow the tarmac road back to the car park.

10. White Hill

This walk climbs to the mast on Windy Hill from the reservoirs in the Piethorne Valley and then follows the Pennine Way southwards taking in White Hill and Millstone Edge before dropping down to the road at Standedge. The route then passes the Castleshaw Reservoirs, climbs the moors and heads north again, passing the Readycon Dean Reservoir before descending back into the Piethorne Valley. It is a strenuous moorland traverse and map and compass may be necessary in poor conditions. It also links with Walk 9 (Blackstone Edge) and Walk 11 (Crompton Moor) giving opportunities for longer walks.

Peaks and Panoramas: The route follows the main Pennine ridge along the Pennine Way and takes in, from north to south, WINDY HILL, GREEN HOLE HILL, WHITE HILL, RAPE HILL and MILLSTONE EDGE. Windy Hill, White Hill and Millstone Edge stand out as the three main peaks and all provide far-reaching views from west to east, from Greater Manchester over to Yorkshire. Windy Hill is easy to recognise by its stout mast (see also Walk 9), the grassy summit of White Hill has a triangulation pillar and so does Millstone Edge which also has interesting rock formations and a gritstone edge running north to Northern Rotcher. This edge gives a good view south along the Tame Valley. There is also a memorial to the dialect poet Ammon Wrigley close to the summit of Millstone Edge. The walk also runs below BROADHEAD NODDLE which overlooks the Castleshaw Reservoirs.

Distance: 14½ miles

Maps: Ordnance Survey Pathfinder Number 701 Bury, Rochdale and Littleborough; Ordnance Survey Pathfinder Number 702 Huddersfield; Ordnance Survey Outdoor Leisure Sheet 1 The Peak District (Dark Peak Area)

Start: Piethorne Valley car park, Ogden Reservoir, Ogden Lane, Newhey (Grid Reference 953 123).

Getting there: From Newhey take the A640 Huddersfield Road and follow it uphill, past the train station, for about a mile until a little lane branching off it to the left is reached. This is Ogden Lane – turn down it and continue along it after the sign for 'Private Road' is reached. The car park is on the left just after the dam of the first reservoir, Ogden Reservoir, is reached and there is an information board, toilets and ranger's office adjacent to it.

Public transport: Go to Newhey by bus from Rochdale or travel by train to the station on Huddersfield Road. From Newhey, walk up Huddersfield Road and turn down Ogden Lane as above. The journey from Newhey to the Ogden Reservoir and return will add approximately two and a half miles to the total route above.

Background

The Ogden Valley or the Piethorne Valley – it is known by both names – contains six Victorian reservoirs which were constructed between 1858 and 1901 to supply water to Oldham, Rochdale and Chadderton. The catchment waters of the reservoirs flow down from Bleakedgate Moor mainly via the two steep valleys of Piethorne Clough and Cold Greave Clough and the former stream rises just below the radio mast on top of Windy Hill. Piethorne was the first reservoir to be completed, in 1866, and the others were added as demand for water grew from the expanding nearby towns. Many of the fine stone houses along Ogden Lane were associated with the reservoirs but Ogden was a farming and textile settlement before the valley was flooded and many of the old farmsteads lie in ruins. Note also the little graveyard of the Ogden Baptist Chapel, almost hidden on the right-hand side of Ogden Lane as you approach the reservoirs from the Newhey end.

On the high tops above Piethorne runs the famous Pennine Way, two little words synonymous with northern rambling which have come to symbolise all the passion, pain, stamina and challenge involved in long-distance walking. It was the brainchild of a rambling enthusiast,

The Pennine Way to Millstone Edge

Tom Stephenson, now sadly deceased, who was inspired by the American example of the Appalachian Trail and suggested the idea for a route along the backbone of England as early as 1935. It took 30 years for his plan to come to fruition and the Pennine Way officially opened in 1965 as a 270-mile route from Edale to Kirk Yetholm – the first long distance path in the country. The P.W. will also forever be associated with that other hiking legend, Alfred Wainwright, who promised a drink for all who completed the trail at the Border Hotel in Kirk Yetholm. Wainwright could not have imagined how many would take up his offer! As you are only walking a tiny fraction of the P.W. in this hike, I shall treat you to an ice cube (only one, mind) in the Ram's Head.

Ammon Wrigley (1861-1946) was the Saddleworth equivalent of the Rochdale dialect poet, Edwin Waugh, who is commemorated at Waugh's Well in the Rossendale hills (see Walk 6). Wrigley has his own memorial stone on Millstone Edge, which looks down on his beloved country. His ashes were also scattered here in 1946, over the prominent rock formation known as the Dinner Stone.

Roman garrisons did their own version of the Pennine Way in the First Century when they marched between Deva, Mamucium and Eboracum, or rather Chester, Manchester and York as they are better known today. Governor Agricola was preparing a military push into Scotland and brought his sun-tanned boys into the wilds of upland Brigantia where a string of forts were built along the road to service their activities. Castleshaw was one such minor resting place and the fort here, close to the site of the present reservoirs, was built soon after AD 79 and was probably abandoned 50 years later as the Romans moved north to Scotland under Hadrian. He built his wall and the rest, as they say, is history.

This walk also plods along another of the many pre-turnpike packhorse routes that radiated out of Rochdale, the centre of Lancashire's woollen trade, and crossed the Pennines into Yorkshire. The Rapes Highway ran via Littleborough to Marsden and passed under Rape Hill – the tracks above Piethorne and around the Readycon Dean reservoir are part of this old route. The Long Causeway (see Walk 8) and the Blackstone Edge road (see Walk 9) are other examples of preserved packhorse trading routes.

The Route

1. Go out of the car park entrance and immediately cross the stile by the gate on the right, which leads up to the dam of Ogden Reservoir. Walk along the dam and, at the end of it, climb the steps which lead up to a gap in the wall. Turn right here and follow the track above the reservoir, which passes through a kissing gate and then leaves the reservoir behind and runs between a plantation and a little brook. When a T-junction of paths is soon reached at a stone waymarker, turn right and cross the brook to climb stone steps. Continue straight ahead between the walls and another track is joined. Turn left onto this and follow the track gradually uphill, keeping a little wooded valley on your left. At the top of the valley, look out for a waymarker stone with a yellow arrow on the left and turn off the track here to follow a path through rough pasture down to a walled enclosure. Bear diagonally right from here and climb up to the boundary wall to reach a step-stile in the wall – this is difficult to see until you are right next to it. Cross this and turn right along the track to pass through a bridlegate to a crossroads of paths overlooking the nearby M62 and Hollingworth Lake.

2. Continue straight ahead along the stone track, which passes under pylons. The track becomes a very boggy sunken lane between walls, though an alternative drier route has developed just above it to the right. Keep going straight ahead and the knolls of Nicholas Pike and Town Hill rise on either side. Eventually, the wide track, part of the Rapes Highway, comes to a junction of routes where there is a profusion of blue waymarkers. The track forks here, take the fork turning sharp left and the boggy track continues uphill between walls. The track is followed up a distinct ridge for the next one and a half miles and leads straight to the triangular mast on Windy Hill. Just keep a wall on the left and aim directly for the triangular mast; as it is neared, the track becomes steeper. Pass the mast on the right and join the access road. Do not go all the way down to the 'A' road but turn right along the path running left to right, to reach the main road (between Denshaw and Ripponden) slightly further up. You are now on the Pennine Way long-distance footpath and also on the boundary between Lancashire and Yorkshire (well, metropolitan Greater Manchester and West Yorkshire).

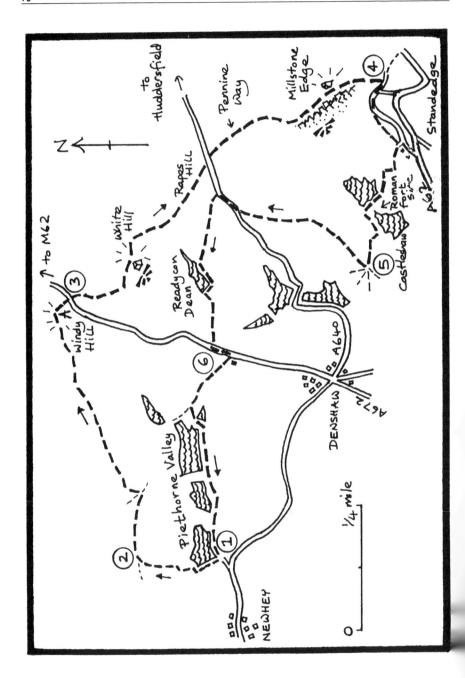

3. The walk trudges along the Pennine Way for the next five miles from Windy Hill to the road at Standedge and is easy to follow, due to its heavy use. The first objective is White Hill, the highest point on the walk. Cairns lead up to the summit triangulation pillar along the ridge of Axletree Edge and Green Hole Hill. The route then runs over the flat-topped plateau of Rapes Hill and descends along a grassy path to the Huddersfield Road, which has come up from Denshaw. Turn left and cross the road, picking up the continuation of the Pennine Way almost opposite below a small car parking area. There is a National Trust sign for Marsden Moor here; the way continues over a footbridge and along a path with an artificial surface. There are good views east and west from this path and it eventually reaches a stone waymarker, erected in 1996, from where there is a good view south to Saddleworth. Turn left at the waymarker and climb up to the rock outcrops overlooking the Castleshaw Reservoirs. The edge of the rocky escarpment is followed for the next mile to reach the triangulation pillar on the top of Millstone Edge, with the Ammon Wrigley memorial stone adjacent to it. From here, descend to the unfenced track above Standedge but do not follow it down to the A62 road.

4. Instead, turn right along the track that runs parallel to the busy road below it and becomes a wide lane. When it swings left and starts to drop down to the road, look out for a bridleway, waymarked as the Standedge Trail, which continues straight ahead through a gate on the right-hand side of the lane. Join this track for about a third of a mile; shortly after it rejoins the lane, turn sharp right down an adjoining lane which passes houses and meanders down to the two Castleshaw Reservoirs which can be seen below. When the lane forks near the reservoir edge, take the right fork leading along the dam of the upper reservoir. The site of the Roman fort is in the pastures over to the left, overlooking the lower reservoir. At the end of the dam turn right along the track for approximately 200 metres then, ignoring the footpath which continues straight ahead, turn sharp right up a walled track which climbs steeply uphill to a crossroads of moorland tracks. The steeply rising hill to the right of the track is Broadhead Noddle.

5. There is a metal waymarker signpost at the crossroads which was erected by the Ramblers Association in 1985 to celebrate its 50th anniversary and renewed in 1994. Turn right here and follow the track

signed for the Pennine Way which climbs uphill and keeps just below the highest point of Broadhead Noddle. After half a mile, the
track reaches a boundary wall and then continues uphill as a faint
path across the open moor and towards a cairn. Below, to the left,
can be seen the Dowry and New Year's Bridge Reservoirs on either
side of the main road running down into Denshaw village. The path
keeps halfway up the hillside and eventually joins the road by a footpath signpost. Turn right up the road for approximately 300 metres
until a gated track is reached on the left-hand side of the road. Cross
the stile and join this track, which is followed for the next one and a
half miles across lonely moorland and past the isolated Readycon
Dean Reservoir before reaching a main road. The track, another section of the Rapes Highway, is easy to follow, at first running below
Rape Hill then swinging left alongside the reservoir and crossing its
dam. On the far side of the dam turn left and the track runs above a
steep sided clough, passes through two bridle gates, and reaches the
Ripponden Road.

6. On the far side of the road there is a good view across to the
Rossendale Hills and West Pennine Moors – Knowl Hill, Peel Tower
and the Winter Hill masts may be visible. The Piethorne Valley can
also be seen much closer at hand. Turn left and take care, following
the road downhill for approximately 300 metres until the Ram's
Head Inn is reached on the right. Join the signed bridleway along the
track between the pub and outbuildings and follow it for the next
half a mile down into the Piethorne Valley. The stony track crosses a
drain and drops down more steeply as the reservoirs are neared. Do
not drop all the way down to Piethorne Reservoir but look out for a
waymarker stone with blue and white arrows alongside the track.
Take the adjoining track, which forks left at the stone and runs between walls, soon swinging left across the dam of a smaller reservoir
(Hanging Lees). Keep to the wide track, which turns sharp right on
the far side of the dam and is followed for the next mile back to the
car park at Ogden. Keep the reservoirs on the right and the track
eventually joins a tarmac access road. Pass the water treatment
works and some interesting Victorian houses dating from the time'
the reservoirs were built. After passing the ranger station, the car
park is reached on the right.

11. Crompton Moor

This walk explores the upper reaches of the River Tame and climbs the ridges on both sides of the valley between Denshaw and Grains Bar. The walk drops down to the river before climbing up to an old moorland road across Ox Hey Top. The route passes through Denshaw, Saddleworth's most northerly village, before following the high eastern edge of Crompton Moor which overlooks the Tame Valley and Oldham Road. It also links with Walk 10 (White Hill) and Walk 12 (Slades Rocks) giving opportunities for longer walks.

Peaks and Panoramas: OX HEY TOP is a broad ridge at the northern end of Saddleworth which separates the Tame Valley from the Castleshaw Reservoirs. It is traversed by an old moorland road running north from Delph, known as Broad Lane. Facing it, on the west side of the Tame, is the steep sided edge of TAME SCOUT, the highest part of a large moorland mass known as CROMPTON MOOR, which shelters Shaw and Crompton village. Crompton Moor, with its triangulation pillar, is easy to identify as it is topped by three masts of different height. The ridges on both sides of the Tame offer extensive views across Saddleworth and the obelisks at Pots and Pans and Bishop's Park are easy to spot. They also look east to the Yorkshire Pennines, north to Windy Hill and Blackstone Edge and Tame Scout provides a prospect south to the urban scene of Oldham and the city centre. Ox Hey Top overlooks the Castleshaw Reservoirs and provides a view of the site of the Roman fort that once stood here.

Distance: 6½ miles

Map: Ordnance Survey Pathfinder Number 701 Bury, Rochdale and Littleborough; Ordnance Survey Outdoor Leisure Sheet 1 The Peak District (Dark Peak Area)

Start: Bishop Park car park, Halifax Road, Grains Bar (Grid Reference 962 085).

Getting there: The main entrance to Bishop Park (owned by Oldham M.B.C.) is reached on the A672 between Oldham and Denshaw. It is signposted from this road close to the Grains Bar crossroads by the King's Arms. The Park has an alternative car park (Grid Reference 967 083) closer to the Bishop Monument on the other side of the pitch and putt course. This is reached via Ship Lane which forks right behind the King's Arms.

Public transport: A bus service between Oldham and Halifax stops on Halifax Road at the entrance to Bishop Park, Grains Bar.

Background

Grains Bar is at the head of several forking valleys or 'grains' and stands almost upon a moorland pass which separates old world Saddleworth from the urban sprawl of Oldham and Shaw. At a crossroads on the Oldham-Ripponden turnpike road, the 'bar' was the toll-bar on the route north to Denshaw and the former toll house still stands on the corner. Also on the corner of Buckstones Road is an old black and white road sign erected by the long forgotten Crompton Urban District Council.

Overlooked by Grains Bar is the young Tame Valley. The river flows through a pleasant rural stretch between Denshaw and Delph, enclosed by steep slopes upon which Oldham Road and Denshaw Road run parallel on opposite sides of the valley. The river has to make the most of its moorland tranquillity, for within a few miles it hits Mossley and Stalybridge and is transformed into the urban-industrial waterway that gave rise to the many towns that collectively take the name, Tameside. It has no respite, for in Stockport town centre it joins the River Goyt and forms the River Mersey and does not get any fresh air again until Cheshire. The actual source of the River Tame is on the high slopes of White Hill, three miles to the north of Denshaw. Pennine Way walkers cross the cloughs that carry the streams down to a series of reservoirs along the Huddersfield Road and the Tame begins as the reservoir outlet. It is also fed from the springs upon Black Hill which flow down into the Greenfield Valley further south.

Denshaw marks the beginning of Saddleworth and grew up as a settlement at a crossroads of several packhorse routes linked to the woollen trade between Lancashire and Yorkshire. These tracks were later turnpiked and in the 18th century most of the present-day village developed and the Junction Inn became an important halt for stagecoaches. The Romans were, of course, much earlier travellers through Saddleworth and a fort was built at Castleshaw where the reservoirs now stand. Built around AD79 it only had a brief period of use as a resting place for troops on the route from Manchester to York (see also Walk 10).

Places of rest and refreshment for modern day travellers include La Pergola Hotel and Restaurant and the Alpine Restaurant and Bistro on the Rochdale Road rising out of Denshaw village. In a windswept backwater, they bring an unexpected flavour of continental Europe to the old turnpike road.

The Route

1. From Bishop Park car park walk back to the Grains Bar junction between the Kings Arms and Boars Head pubs. Walk along the main road, Oldham Road, just past the junction and look for a public footpath signpost on the right-hand side of the road in front of the Grains Bar B & B. Join this path which becomes a grass track behind outbuildings and runs downhill between fences. It reaches a walled track which bears left to a white house, do not take this but instead bear right across the hillside along a boggy path between a wall, on the left, and newly planted trees. The path keeps above the valley, which runs north towards Denshaw, but slightly descends a steep heather hillside along a path which can be slippery when wet. The path skirts around the hillside and looks across to a church on the side of Ox Hey Top, soon reaching a gap in a wall close to pylons. Swing left here and follow the path under the pylons with the wall on the left. Pass trees and reach a walled lane by gateposts, close to a farmhouse on the right.

2. The path becomes difficult to find at this point but just continue in the same direction, keeping below the farmhouse but maintaining the same height to pass between mature and newly planted trees. A stone gate post is reached and the path becomes clearer now and runs downhill to another stone post and then to a large sycamore tree. Turn right and follow a track above a steep-sided woodland to reach a gate and stile. Cross this and drop down to the river, almost turning back on yourself to reach another gate and stile leading to a footbridge over the stream which is, in fact, the infant River Tame. It will be crossed again before the walk is over. On the far side of the bridge continue along the track between hedges which becomes a wide gravel track running through woodland to reach a collection of farm buildings. The track swings sharp right between the houses and follows the concrete driveway uphill to a turreted entrance by a road. Cross the road, running between Denshaw and Delph, and continue straight ahead along a field edge to reach a narrow lane at the end of a row of cottages.

3. Turn right and follow the lane past the cottages and there are views ahead to the War Memorial on Pots and Pans and right to the obelisk on Bishop Park. Keep to the lane for quarter of a mile until it reaches a wooden footpath signpost on the left by a gate with a 'Private Road – Footpath Only' sign. Join this path which leads up a walled track

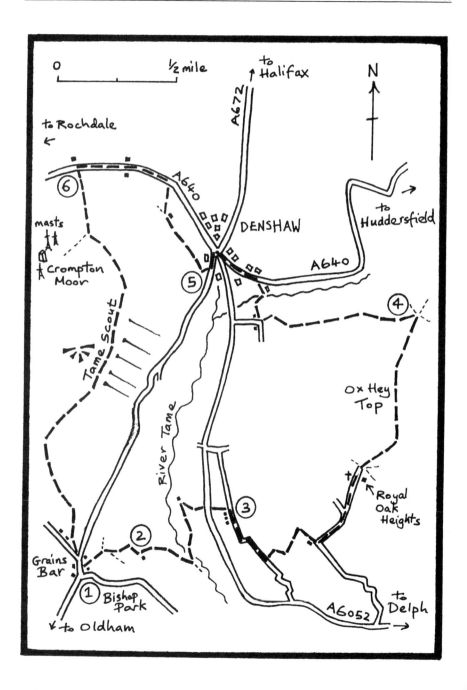

between fields and heads towards the church on the hill. Look left for a view of the edge of Crompton Moor which has pylons crossing over it. The walled track passes through another gate then turns sharp right and passes along the side of a long barn to reach another lane beyond a gate. Turn left along this lane and follow it uphill to reach the lonely church and graveyard and the Royal Oak Heights pub. Continue straight ahead along the lane, Broad Lane, which is followed over Ox Hey Top for the next mile. Stick to the main route heading north – ignore paths leaving the lane on either side. The tarmac ends and the old route becomes a wide walled track overlooking the Castleshaw Reservoirs. The Roman fort stood on the spur of land on the far side of the lower reservoir. The track eventually begins to drop downhill to a crossroads of tracks by a metal waymarker signpost originally erected by the Ramblers Association in 1985.

4. Turn left here and follow the wide track signposted for Denshaw. The village can be glimpsed over to the right and facing you, on the far side of the valley, is Tame Scout on the edge of Crompton Moor. Follow the track, known as Ox Hey Lane, for about three-quarters of a mile. It becomes tarmac beyond a gate and drops down to meet a lane signed as Wham Lane. Leave the lane here by joining a signed footpath on the right of the lane junction. This overgrown path runs in front of a house and drops downhill along a field edge, bearing right to cross the River Tame again. Follow the track uphill and bear

The Heights

left up the lane, Wall Green, past houses to reach the Huddersfield Road. Turn left and follow this 'A' road past the parish church and the post office to arrive at the busy junction of roads overlooked by the Junction Inn in the centre of Denshaw village. Turn down the second road on the left of the junction, the A672, signed as Oldham Road, and follow it for approximately 150 metres until a footpath signpost is reached on the right.

5. Join this path, which climbs up a grass bank and follows a drive between two houses. Turn right along the track between the houses and pass another property, continuing straight ahead along a path which climbs the hillside and overlooks a main road leading out of Denshaw. The path heads towards a farmhouse further along the hillside and, when it is reached, turn right between the buildings and follow the track downhill to meet the road at a cattle grid. The road is the Rochdale Road which leads over the hill to Newhey. Follow it uphill for nearly half a mile past a hotel on the right and a restaurant on the left. Eventually, Rochdale M.B.C. road signs are reached where footpath signs lead off on either side of the highway. There is also a house on the right-hand side of the road which was formerly the Moorcock Inn.

6. Turn left by the locked gate and join the path which follows a tarmac access road uphill to a waymarker signpost. The access road continues to the masts, but you take the track forking left off it, which is waymarked as the Crompton Circuit. This goes through a gate and the track runs along the edge, marked on the map as Boothstead Edge, with the fence to your left. Look back for a good view north along the Pennines and over to Rochdale. The three masts of Crompton Moor lie over to your right but they are not very pretty and the view to them is further spoiled by the line of pylons. Instead, we stick to the edge, Tame Scout, and follow it for the next one and a half miles back to Grains Bar. Two tracks run parallel along the first part of the edge, a sunken path nearer the boundary on the left and a wide stony track. Both head in the same direction and soon bear left to reach the highest point of the moor as the views open out looking southwards and take in Oldham, Hartshead Pike and the city centre. Keep to the boundary wall and drop downhill to pass under the line of pylons and head straight towards the city. When the track swings sharp right, leave it and continue straight ahead along the wall-side. A field-edge path crosses stiles and soon brings you out at the Grains Bar junction by the Boars Head.

12. Slades Rocks

This strenuous walk follows quiet lanes and paths across numerous moorland edges upon the west and east sides of the Upper Tame Valley. Between the hills the walk climbs down to the valley settlements of Uppermill, Diggle and Delph. It links with Walk 10 (White Hill), Walk 11 (Crompton Moor) and Walk 13 (Alderman's Hill) giving opportunities for much longer walks.

Peaks and Panoramas: There are extensive views along most of the route starting straight away by looking from the triangulation pillar and monument at BISHOP PARK towards the Manchester conurbation. WHARMTON HILL has a commanding position over the Tame Valley above Grasscroft and is easy to recognise by its rounded shape and TV mast. From Wharmton there are views south towards Mossley and Stalybridge and east to the Peak District National Park. SLADES ROCKS are the highest point reached on the walk and lie along the southern spur of flat-topped BROADSTONE HILL, not accessible by right of way. Facing these rock outcrops on the opposite side of the Tame Valley is HARROP EDGE, a lower ridge traversed by an old highway. Slades Rocks and Harrop Edge offer views of upper Saddleworth villages. The final leg of the walk follows a lane along the slopes of BADGER EDGE which looks north to Denshaw and the source of the River Tame.

Distance: 14 miles

Map: Ordnance Survey Outdoor Leisure Sheet 1: The Peak District (Dark Peak Area)

Start: Bishop Park car park, Halifax Road, Grains Bar (Grid Reference 962 085).

Getting there: The main entrance to Bishop Park (owned by Oldham M.B.C.) is reached on the A672 between Oldham and Denshaw. It is signposted from this road close to the Grains Bar crossroads by the King's Arms. The Park has an alternative car park (Grid Reference 967 083) closer to the Bishop Monument on the other side of the pitch and putt course. This is reached via Ship Lane which forks right behind the King's Arms.

Public transport: A bus service between Oldham and Halifax stops on Halifax Road at the entrance to Bishop Park, Grain Bar.

Background

Driving up from Oldham and dropping down into Saddleworth at Grains Bar was always a bit like falling off the edge of the modern world and stumbling into the land that time forgot. It was a Yorkshire Shangri-La existing beyond the clouds of urban life. It still is in many ways, but a new breed of Daihatsu-driving, cottage-renovating commuter is quickly transforming this Lost Horizon into just another suburb.

The narrow roads and green lanes encountered on this walk were not built to accommodate 4x4 jeeps looking for the quickest way on to the M62. I blame Victor Pendlebury, Mavis Riley's boyfriend in 'Coronation Street' who, in 1983, put Saddleworth on the map by leaving the grim terraces of Weatherfield and buying a stone cottage here to concentrate on his poetry.

Saddleworth was an ancient parish and pre-1974 formed an urban district in the West Riding of Yorkshire. Its numerous villages and hamlets (often referred to as 'folds') became a focus for domestic weaving along the upper reaches of the River Tame and its tributaries. As a result, the movement of cloth over the Pennines created an intricate web of packhorse roads radiating out of the valleys and along the moorland ridges. Of course, the River Tame flows south from here and helped to industrialise Stalybridge, Ashton, Dukinfield, Denton and Hyde before joining the River Goyt at Stockport to form the mighty River Mersey.

The villages of Uppermill, Diggle and Delph, passed through on this walk, prospered from domestic weaving. They were also given an impetus to growth by later transport developments, namely, the turnpiking of roads, the opening of the Huddersfield Narrow Canal and the building of a railway through the Tame Valley. The canal ran for 20 miles from Ashton and Stalybridge to Huddersfield and was built between 1794 and 1811. It took so long to build because it required the cutting of a tunnel deep under the Pennine grits and shales at Standedge. This was the longest (3 miles), highest and most expensive canal tunnel in the country; it begins at Diggle, not re-emerging until Marsden in Yorkshire. The tunnel was also utilised by the railway line from Stalybridge to Huddersfield which opened in 1849 and created an alternative link between Manchester and Leeds. In fact, three railway lines were cut under Standedge and were used in early tests for a Channel Tunnel.

Slades Rocks are part of a line of rock outcrops and natural stone curiosities that extend south to the Pots and Pans obelisk and Alderman's Hill. To the north and west, the featureless rough pasture stretches away to Broadstone Hill and bleak Saddleworth Moor. Below Slades Rocks is Pobgreen, a typical example of an old weaving hamlet and, below this, is the 13th century Saddleworth parish church, probably the oldest surviving building in the valley. One other monument worthy of note is the Bishop family obelisk which stands on a hill at Bishop Park and offers panoramic views. The park takes its name from the Bishop family, who donated the land to the public and built the monument in honour of William and Anne Bishop. It is certainly a panoramic but blustery spot for pitch and putt.

Harrop Edge Lane is a straight ridge road above the Castleshaw Reservoirs, which was part of a Roman highway between the fort at Castleshaw and the fort further south at Glossop in Longdendale. Another section of it is walked in Walk 14.

Uppermill viaduct and the Huddersfield Canal

The Route

1. From the car park by the tourist information board, go through the gateway leading to a stone building. Turn immediately left and follow the path along the wall-side, signed as a bridleway and the Medlock Valley Way. The path leads to the road adjacent to the King's Arms. Turn right and almost immediately take the right fork up Ship Lane. This leads to another car park on your right overlooking the pitch and putt course. In the far corner of the car park, go through the pedestrian access (signed as the Medlock Valley Way) and follow the distinct path up the hill to the Bishop Monument. From here, there are excellent views in all directions, including the nearby village of Delph, but most strikingly towards Oldham and Manchester. Follow the path which leads past the nearby triangulation pillar and down the other side of the hill, bearing slightly left, then right, and crossing stiles to join a lane.

2. Turn right on this lane and follow it southwards for approximately three-quarters of a mile, heading in the direction of suburban Oldham. It eventually meets a junction of roads by the Roebuck Inn, where you turn sharp left and join Whitegates Lane. Shortly before the junction is reached, a signed footpath on the left crosses a field corner and joins Whitegates Lane, cutting off the junction. Follow Whitegates Lane south-eastwards for just over half a mile until it passes the entrance to High Moor Quarry by a crossroads. Do not turn right but continue straight ahead along the signed footpath that runs to the rear of cottage gardens on the right. This leads to a stile and gate by the corner of a wall. Go through this and immediately turn right, following the wall-side downhill to meet a lane.

3. On the opposite side of the lane, cross the stile and continue directly ahead in the same southward direction. Follow the field edge with the wall immediately on your right through two fields until another road, the busier A62, is reached. Continue straight ahead on the opposite side of the road, going through a gate and following the wall-side path through several fields. A number of stiles are crossed and the path leaves the wall behind, becoming a faint grass path which climbs gradually uphill, to the right of overgrown quarry workings. Keep walking in the same direction as the path goes over the brow of a hill, through a gate and joins a driveway between two properties leading down to a residential lane. Turn right and follow

this lane (Burnedge Lane) for just over a quarter of a mile until a signed footpath is reached on the right-hand side of the lane almost opposite Burnedge Bent Farm.

4. Leave the lane and take this path, following an access track heading eastward with Wharmton TV mast visible to your right. When the track meets the corner of a wall, continue downhill, keeping the wall on your left. The obelisk on 'Pots and Pans' can be seen almost directly ahead on the moors on the opposite side of the valley. The path soon drops down to a stile between a golf course and an old quarry. Cross this and go down the track to meet a narrow lane. The path continues downhill on the opposite side of the lane and quickly meets a railway (Manchester-Huddersfield-Leeds line). Beware of trains and cross the railway, continuing downhill to meet a lane. Turn sharp right and the lane crosses over the Huddersfield Narrow Canal. The route continues along the canal towpath but Uppermill village (with craft shops, tea rooms, pub and museum) is worth a look and can be reached by continuing along the lane which joins the High Street. Turn left and join the canal towpath next to a row of pretty cottages. Follow the pleasant towpath for nearly half a mile until the Brownhills visitor centre (a stone building with steps) is reached on your right, shortly after crossing under a railway viaduct which dates from the 1840s.

5. Go up the steps and pass through the entrance to the centre to reach the road (A670). Climb the narrow lane on the opposite side of the road, which goes under the railway viaduct and runs uphill to houses. When the lane swings sharp left, continue straight ahead along the tarmac path between houses. When the path forks, again go straight ahead along a narrow fenced path with a field to your left and gardens to your right. The path soon meets a drive, bear left along the drive and cross a disused railway. The drive then forks; take the right fork (avoiding the private driveway) and the path becomes a pleasant track with a holly hedge and wall to your left. Follow the path for half a mile, heading towards the church tower which can be high on the hillside almost directly ahead. The path at first follows the wall-side, then passes through a number of field enclosures before crossing a brook and climbing stone steps to emerge on a lane behind the church yard. Turn right and follow the lane around to the front of the interesting parish church of St. Chad's.

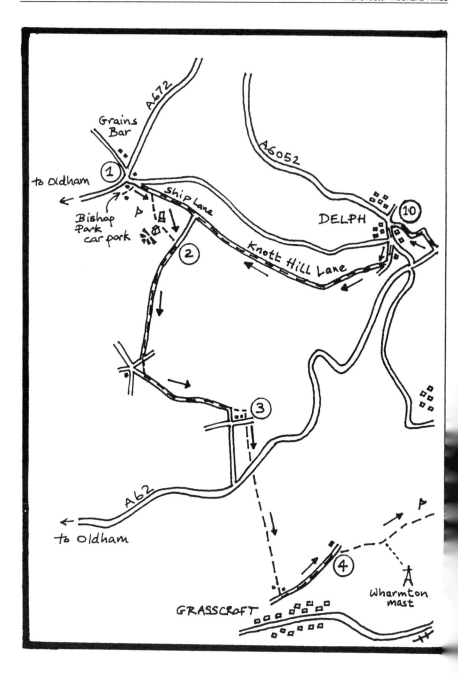

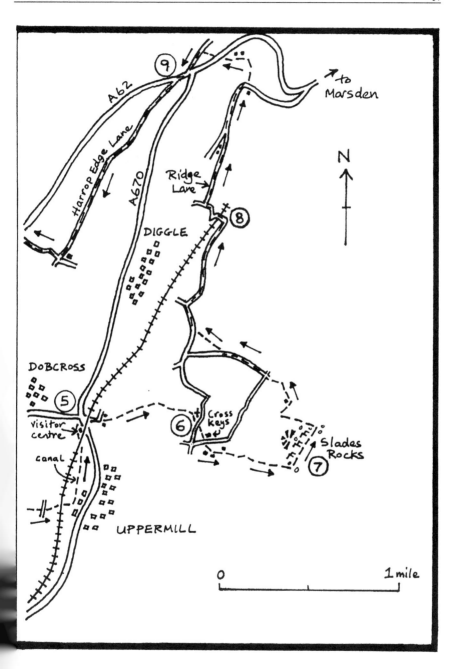

6. Look for a path signed for a pub on the far side of the lane in front of the church. Follow this uphill through a field to emerge in the car park of the Cross Keys Inn. Climb the steps on the far side of the car park to join a lane. Almost opposite is Pobgreen Lane; follow this uphill until Hawthorn Cottage is reached on the right. Next to this, look for a signed footpath leading up some steps and follow this grass track straight ahead, climbing steeply between walls. The walk has now entered the Peak District National Park (at least for the next mile or so). Another cottage is reached on the left, behind this cross the stile and the path becomes a wide green track bearing slightly left, then slightly right before heading directly up the moor with a wall on your left. The sunken track becomes less distinct but go straight up to the top of the moor, bearing slightly left near the top as the path swings around through two gateposts to reach the prominent crags of Slades Rocks. There are good views in all directions here, including the bleak expanse of Saddleworth Moor, Hartshead Pike, Manchester, Oldham and the Bishop Monument. The large TV transmitter (with lights) to be seen directly to the east is at Holme Moss above Holmfirth.

7. With the crags and wall on your left, continue walking in the same direction, north-westwards, until the path drops down to a signpost with Oldham Way waymarkers. Turn left and follow the wide green track steeply downhill, heading back in the direction of the church. When the slope becomes more gradual, look for a stile and gate in the wall to your right. Cross the stile and follow the walled path, which bears left to reach the corner of a derelict barn. Just to the right of the barn, go through the gap in a wall and head diagonally right across the field to the opposite corner and a stile. Cross this and follow the stone track downhill to reach a lane crossroads. Continue in the same direction down Running Hill Lane and, almost immediately after passing some upmarket cottages, look out for a green track (not signed as a right of way) which forks right from the lane. Follow this downhill in the direction of Diggle village. The track rejoins a lane; turn right along the lane and follow it northwards. Minor roads are followed for the next mile and a half. Soon, when the lane forks, take the right fork and walk in the direction of the valley head until the lane swings sharp left over a railway line close to the Diggle Hotel. Just north of the road bridge, both the canal and railway disappear under the famous Standedge Tunnels.

8. Cross the road bridge and turn right up Harrop Court Road, then almost immediately turn sharp left up a steep tarmac path with a bollard to rejoin a lane. Walk directly ahead towards a pleasant green surrounded by cottages and turn sharp right up Ridge Lane. This narrow, hedged lane climbs Harrop Ridge above the upper reaches of the Tame Valley which can be seen to your right. When the lane eventually joins another minor road at the Old Toll House, continue climbing uphill in the same direction until the road bends right. At this point, join a tarmac access track, signed as a bridleway, which can be seen on the far side of the bend heading northwards. This track soon swings left past cottages, crossing a beck that is a moorland tributary of the infant River Tame. After passing Dean Head Farm take the right fork of the track which joins the A62 (Oldham-Huddersfield) road. Go directly across the road to follow a green track leading to a minor lane. Turn left down here and the A62 is soon rejoined. There are grand views of Saddleworth from this point. Turn right and follow the busy A62 for approximately 180 metres until Harrop Edge Lane is reached on the opposite side of the road.

9. This rough tarmac lane is marked by an old Saddleworth U.D.C. sign and leads over a minor hill identified on O.S. maps as Hunters Hill. It is followed in a generally south-south-west direction for the next mile and a quarter, running straight along the long spur of Harrop Edge and is thought to be the route of a Roman road. The actual summit of the edge is just to the left of the lane, close to some farm buildings. Delph village comes into view on the right and Bishop Monument (our final destination) is also seen – looking miles and miles away! When an isolated stone house is eventually reached on the left, at a crossroads of tracks, turn right and drop down steeply from the ridge along a rough stone lane. This leads down towards Delph and soon meets the A62 again. Cross the main road and almost directly opposite join the narrow Rumbles Lane. Follow this residential lane for nearly half a mile as it passes a cricket ground, swings sharp left then right around the hillside before joining the High Street at Delph close to a church.

10. Turn left on reaching the main street and walk through the village crossing the river and passing characterful shops and pubs. When you reach a junction of three roads at the top of the street, ignore the road joining on the right, Grains Road, but continue straight ahead taking the lane (Stoneswood Road) which forks to the right and leads uphill past a mixture of old and new cottages. The village is soon left behind and the lane swings right and forks again. Take the right fork, signed as Knott Hill Lane, which runs uphill between garages and the rear of a row of cottages. This hedged lane climbs uphill, almost forever, and runs just below the top of Badger Edge which offers distant views northward to Windy Hill and Blackstone Edge. Follow the lane for about a mile and a half until the car park below the Bishop Monument is passed on the left. Retrace your steps to the Bishop Park car park.

13. Alderman Hill

This walk involves a steep climb but is essentially a potter around the interesting rock formations and viewpoints of the moorland ridge above the Tame Valley, ending dramatically in the shear drop of Alderman Hill. From Dovestone Reservoir the walk climbs gradually above the valley before a steep ascent to the obelisk on Pots and Pans. Various rock formations are explored before heading for Alderman Hill, after which a green lane leads to a gentle descent along the reservoir edge. This walk is best enjoyed during a quieter part of the week (not weekends) when you will have time to potter around the Pots and Pans and the reservoir without too many crowds. It links with Walk 12 (Slades Rocks) and Walk 14 (Hoarstone Edge) giving opportunities for longer walks.

Peaks and Panoramas: POTS AND PANS has a war memorial, easily the most recognisable and popular viewpoint in the whole of Saddleworth. This part of the ridge overlooking the Greenfield Valley takes its name from the weird rock formations surrounding the obelisk, one of which resembles pots and pans. The obelisk erected to the war dead of local villages looks west across east Manchester and beyond. Heading north the ridge becomes the rather featureless plateau of DICK HILL, only enlivened by curious rock formations, outcrops and deposits such as the Kinder Stones, Oven Stones, Shaw Rocks and the Sugar Loaf. To the south, the ridge ends in the craggy shelf of ALDERMAN HILL which gives fine views across Saddleworth Moor and the Chew Valley.

Distance: 6 miles

Map: Ordnance Survey Outdoor Leisure Sheet 1: The Peak District (Dark Peak Area)

Start: Dovestone Reservoir car park, at the end of Bank Lane, Greenfield. (Grid Reference 013 036). Note that this is a Pay and Display car park at weekends but is free of charge during the week.

Getting there: Dovestone Reservoir is reached via the Holmfirth Road (A635) just to the east of Greenfield village. The reservoir is signposted from this road along the narrow Bank Lane which leads down to the dam and car park. There is also a Peak Park ranger station here.

Public transport: There is no bus service to Dovestone Reservoir. However, bus services from Manchester and Oldham stop at the Clarence Hotel, at the roundabout where Manchester Road and Holmfirth Road meet in Greenfield village. From here walk up Holmfirth Road and turn off right when Bank Lane (signed for Dovestone Reservoir) is reached. The return journey from the Clarence Hotel junction to the reservoir car park will add approximately two miles to the total walk route above. Greenfield also has a train station on the Manchester-Huddersfield line. This is on the west side of the village and from here walk all the way through pleasant Greenfield village to join the Holmfirth Road. The return journey from Greenfield station to the reservoir car park will add approximately three and a half miles to the walk length.

Background

This is the classic short Saddleworth walk as it takes in the two most popular viewpoints – the Pots and Pans obelisk and Alderman Hill – and the honeypot of Dovestone Reservoir. The reservoir, built in 1967, shelters beneath the Great and Little Dove Stones and completes the trio of reservoirs which wind down from the moors. The other two – Greenfield and Yeoman Hey – are Victorian in date (see also Walk 14). Dovestone Reservoir is fed from the upland cloughs which fall into Greenfield Brook and the Chew Brook and its outlet meets the River Tame beyond Greenfield. The most easterly tributaries of the Tame rise in the boggy peat groughs close to the summit of Black Hill, once the highest point of Cheshire, but now in Yorkshire.

In Yorkshire legend, 'Alder', translating as the 'high stones', was a giant who fell in love with Rimmon, a nymph of the Chew Brook who married the giant Alphin on the other side of the valley. Alder and Alphin waged a war of rock tossing at each other and Alder killed his neighbour and broken-hearted Rimmon threw herself off the edge. Alder won and Alderman's Hill which bears his name looks decidedly more angry than the gentler spur of Alphin on the other side of Chew Valley. Such legends may have made Alderman Hill popular with ancient druids who are thought to have used the Pots and Pans tablets of stones as their high altars.

Such stones are a common feature of the South Pennine moorlands and are textbook examples of the geomorphic processes of denudation, weathering, erosion and mass-movement. Formations such as the Pots and Pans and the Kinder Stones are gritstone slabs weathered into strange shapes along lines of weakness. Weathered rock fragments are also moved by the forces of water and ice, resulting in curious features like the Sugar Loaf. The grit scarps at the edge of the flat-topped moor, such as Shaw Rocks and Alderman Hill, resemble vertical cliffs because weathering has broken large chunks of rock along straight bedding planes.

Alderman Hill provides views east to the lonely desolation of Saddleworth Moor which has gained unfortunate associations with the

Pots and Pans and War Memorial

1960s Moors Murderers. Ironically, a legacy of murder haunted this area more than a century earlier with the killings at the 'Bill's o' Jacks inn on the Holmfirth Road close to where the plantations can be viewed. It was here, in 1832, that an unknown assailant murdered the innkeeper William Bradbury and his son, Thomas. The legendary inn was demolished in the 1930s.

On a lighter note, it is rather humorous to think that the King of Tonga stood on the dam of Yeoman Hey Reservoir in 1981 and revelled in the delights of Victorian engineering schemes. He placed a stone in the wall to commemorate his visit – which was somewhat out of his way, as he had actually arrived in England to attend the wedding of Prince Charles and Lady Di. He could have been shopping in the West End but the King preferred to experience the wilds of Saddleworth, apparently on the invite of a contractor.

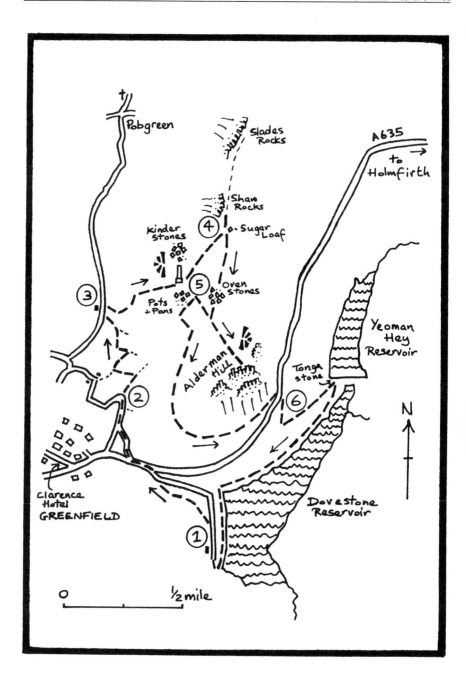

The Route

1. Leave the car park the way you came in and walk back down the road beneath the reservoir dam. Facing you is the main objective of this walk, the high crags of Alderman Hill which has several rocky mounds and a steep east side facing up the valley. Halfway along the length of the dam, turn off Bank Lane via the tarmac road forking off to the left. This leads through woodland and skirts the right-hand side of a mill until shortly a curious revolving gate is reached on the right. Go through this and walk up the cobbled path which swings left to another revolving gate. Continue along the grassy path, diagonally across the hillside to rejoin Bank Lane. Turn left and follow the lane to the A635 Holmfirth Road. Turn left and follow the 'A' road downhill for about 120 metres until the first lane on the right-hand side is reached, signed as Hollins Lane. Cross the road with care and walk up Hollins Lane past the Old Vicarage and when it joins another lane bear right and continue along it for a further 250 metres until it starts to swing left and two footpath signposts are reached on the right-hand side of the lane.

2. Leave the lane at the second signpost which goes through a kissing gate in a wall gap. Follow the grass path straight uphill heading directly towards the Pots and Pans obelisk high above. The pleasant path leads uphill through gorse and hawthorn until, halfway up the hill, a little crossroads of paths is reached alongside the brook to your left. Turn sharp left here and cross the stream via stones to follow a path which bends around the hill and is joined by a semi-derelict wall on the right. It becomes a wide grass path running slightly uphill to a gate and stile. The path then runs between two walls and reaches a farm track. Turn right up the stone track and very shortly take the right fork off it to reach a stile and gate. Continue uphill, heading for the derelict farmstead high above, until another track is soon reached alongside a wall. Turn left and follow this track which passes under telegraph wires. The grass track meanders along a broad shelf and already the valley view reveals Greenfield and Grasscroft, Mossley, Hartshead Pike, Wharmton Hill and Crompton Moor. Continue straight ahead beyond a stile and gate to reach a white-walled farmhouse facing you. Join a lane and pass the farmhouse on the left to reach two footpath signposts on either side of the lane.

3. Take the path on the right, signed for Pots and Pans. The gentle zig-zagging up the hillside is over, and a direct approach to the obelisk is now taken. Follow the sunken path which soon goes through a kissing gate and then climbs steeply to the War Memorial. The view at the top – which includes the city centre and Winter Hill – gives a good excuse for a long breather – use the bench if it is available. Facing directly west across to Wharmton Hill, the Pots and Pans stones, which give the hill its name, lie to the left of the obelisk. They are gnarled by erosion and several precariously balanced tablets of rock help provide a natural frame for the valley view. The walk potters north along the ridge so, to continue the walk, go through the gap in the iron railings – the faint path is waymarked as the Oldham Way. On the left, the fissured rocks known as the Kinder Stones can be seen and the path becomes wide and grassy as it climbs diagonally across the ridge. At the top of the plateau, the path leads left to two interesting boulders marked on the map as Sugar Loaf, presumably because of their resemblance to sugar cubes. The smaller of the rocks is almost completely rounded. Continue north from here to Shaw Rocks, which outcrop on the western edge of the ridge and provide a good view of the Tame Valley.

4. A path continues north from here to link with Walk 12 (Slades Rocks). However, to continue this walk, retrace your steps past the Sugar Loaf and pick out a very faint path heading directly south along the featureless plateau. This path is just to the right of a pipeline indicator and keeps just to the right of the highest point of the ridge, known as Dick Hill. The path soon drops down to the large litter of rocks called the Oven Stones and continue straight ahead from these to pick up a distinct path running left to right across the moor. Turn left along this and follow it for nearly a quarter of a mile along the ridge which ends in the precipitous crags of Alderman Hill. The view across the Greenfield Valley is quite mesmerising with all three reservoirs set within a natural amphitheatre of gritstone edges pierced by high waterfalls. Look up the valley to view the lonely Holmfirth Road winding its weary way over Saddleworth Moor. Not surprisingly, this has been dubbed the 'Isle of Skye' road. You may even be able to pick out your car below the Dovestone dam. The diversion is well worth it, but from here you will have to retrace your steps by following the ridge path just walked along and continuing along it back to the Pots and Pans obelisk.

5. Next to the Pots and Pans stones turn left along a grassy path which swings left and quickly meanders downhill. It drops to a gateway in a wall where there is a stile and an Oldham Way waymarker. Continue straight ahead along the grassy path between two derelict walls and follow it downhill to another gateway and stile by a crossroads of tracks. Turn left at this junction and follow the boggy green lane up the valley for three quarters of a mile, eventually meeting the Holmfirth Road directly under the crags of Alderman Hill. Cross the road and directly opposite turn right to go through the car park of the Binn Green picnic site (remember this useful little car park for future walks). Pass in front of the toilets and, in the corner of the car park, look for a footpath signpost by a litter bin. Take this path between conifers which bears right and drops down a series of steps through a plantation and across a wall gap to join a reservoir access road.

6. Turn left along the access road and follow it downhill, passing through a kissing gate, until the embankment of Yeoman Hey Reservoir is almost reached. The route continues by going through the kissing gate on the right along a track signposted for Dovestone Car Park. Before proceeding, walk to the reservoir wall facing you a bit further along to view the stone laid by his Majesty the King of Tonga in 1981. Continue through the kissing gate to an easy-to-follow surfaced path which skirts the edge of Dovestone Reservoir. The popular path gives good views of the Saddleworth Edges, including Dean and Dove Stone Rocks and Indian's Head above the Chew. The path is followed for the next mile back to the car park and at the corner of the reservoir, go through the gate to continue along the top of the dam to reach the car park at the far end.

14. Hoarstone Edge

This walk starts at the edge of the Peak District National Park and climbs up the wild gorge of the Chew Valley before heading across desolate moorland and descending down Ogden Clough with spectacular views. The route then crosses the lower slopes of Harridge Pike before following an old moorland road above the Tame Valley back to Dovestone Reservoir. The walk is relatively strenuous and a map and compass may be required in misty conditions to traverse Hoarstone Edge, the highest hill in this book. It links with Walk 13 (Alderman Hill) and Walk 16 (Hollingworthall Moor) giving opportunities for longer walks.

Peaks and Panoramas: HOARSTONE EDGE is the highest plateau encountered in this book and sits flat-topped above the craggy ridge on the south side of the Chew Valley. Its extensive views southward and westward encompass the city centre and the eastern side of the Manchester conurbation, Harridge Pike, Hollingworthall and Tintwistle Moors, Longdendale and the high Peak District hills of Bleaklow and Kinder Scout. HARRIDGE PIKE overlooks Mossley and Stalybridge and offers similarly extensive views across these two towns and the eastern side of Manchester. Neither summit is accessible by right of way.

Distance: 11 miles

Map: Ordnance Survey Outdoor Leisure Map No.1 The Peak District (Dark Peak)

Start: Dovestone Reservoir car park, at the end of Bank Lane, Greenfield. (Grid Reference 013 036). Note that this is a Pay and Display car park at weekends but is free of charge during the week.

Getting there: Dovestone Reservoir is reached via the Holmfirth Road (A635) just to the east of Greenfield village. The reservoir is signposted from this road along the narrow Bank Lane which leads down to the dam and car park. There is also a Peak Park ranger station here.

Public transport: There is no bus service to Dovestone Reservoir. But bus services from Manchester and Oldham stop at the Clarence Hotel, at the roundabout where Manchester Road and Holmfirth Road meet in Greenfield village. From here walk up Holmfirth Road and turn off right when Bank Lane (signed for Dovestone Reservoir) is reached. The return journey from the Clarence Hotel junction to the reservoir car park will add approximately 2 miles to the total walk route above.

Greenfield also has a train station on the Manchester-Huddersfield line. This is on the west side of the village and from here walk all the way through pleasant Greenfield village to join the Holmfirth Road. The return journey from Greenfield station to the reservoir car park will add approximately three and a half miles to the walk length.

Dovestones from the Chew Valley road

Background

Greenfield's reservoirs, catching the waters of the fast flowing streams descending from high gritstone edges, are a recreational honeypot. Sailors, climbers and walkers converge here and within a small area you can face various challenges, from walking the easy path around the edge of Dovestone Reservoir, to difficult and death-defying climbs up the vertical slabs of Wimberry Rocks. There are four reservoirs here, which have transformed the converging valleys of Greenfield Brook and Chew Brook: Yeoman Hey (1880), Greenfield (1902), Chew (1912) and Dovestone Reservoir, which was constructed as recently as 1967. Chew Reservoir is the highest constructed in England and stands at 490 metres (1600 feet) above sea level.

But it is the dramatic setting of the reservoirs that makes them the most popular attraction in Saddleworth. The featureless boggy plateaux of Saddleworth Moor, Dove Stone Moss, Featherbed Moss and Hoarstone Edge are flanked by a series of precipitous gritstone edges, rock formations and deep gullies with curious and sinister names such as Charnel Clough, Dish Stone Rocks, Rams Clough and Wilderness. Ancient legends abound in these hidden places and they also record tales of more modern tragedies. Climbers have lost their lives on the crags above the Chew Valley and the Wimberry Rocks (easily identified on the walk up from Dovestone to Chew Reservoir) were the site of a 1949 plane crash in thick mist, when 21 people lost their lives on a flight from Belfast to Manchester.

Wimberry Rocks are also known by the name of Indian's Head due to their resemblance to ... an Indian's Head. Rock boulders, fallen from the weathered and eroded joints of such outcrops, litter the bottom of the Chew Valley but myth suggests that these were the boulders hurled across the valley in anger by the giants Alphin and Alder who were, of course, arguing over a woman – some nymph called Rimmon. The peaks of Alphin and Alderman's Hill face each other on either side of Dovestone Reservoir and take their names from the quarrelsome giants who rest here. (See also Walk 13).

Access issues are never far away from the Peak District National Park, which pioneered the first access agreements to open moorland after it was officially designated in 1951. The battle for walkers' rights was always particularly intense here due to intense recreational pressure from the nearby industrial towns of Lancashire and Yorkshire. Conflict boiled over with the famous Kinder Scout trespass of 1932 which saw five ramblers sent to jail after scuffles with gamekeepers. It was a significant event, which paved the way for future access agreements and legislation in the form of the 1949 National Parks and Access to the Countryside Act The point of this tale is that, despite positive co-operation between the National Park and landowners, many areas are out of bounds at the time of writing. The high ridge on the south side of the Chew Valley, leading from Wilderness to Alphin is a case in point and despite the existence of a track, the home of Alphin the slumbering giant is not accessible by right. However, the existence of a permissive route across Hoarstone Edge to Ogden Clough does at least compensate for this.

Carrbrook is an industrial settlement between Mossley and Stalybridge which has grown up below the massive Buckton Vale Quarry. The quarry cuts into the slopes of Buckton Moor and the ancient site of medieval Buckton Castle, marked on Ordnance Survey maps, is inaccessible. This was, possibly, also a Roman fortress and Moor Edge Road, the old road followed from Carrbrook to the Greenfield Valley, is thought to be part of the Roman highway which linked the forts at Melandra (Glossop) with Castleshaw. See also Walks 10 and 12 for more information on Castleshaw and the Roman road.

The Route

1. From the car park, head uphill to the end of the parking area and follow the tarmac access road which swings left around the south side of the reservoir. Pass the sailing club premises on the left and continue through a kissing gate along the access road which crosses the reservoir inlet. This then swings sharp right, climbing steeply up the hillside overlooking the valley of the Chew Brook. The road is followed up the valley for one and a half miles to reach the dam of Chew Reservoir. Along the way, a stile is crossed marking the boundary of open access and the gorge takes on a Wild West appearance as the menacing crags on either side close in. You sense Red Indians may be looking down on you and note the line of jagged teeth known as Wimberry Rocks (Indian's Head) along the southern ridge. The long slog up the road eventually leads to the dam. Swing right up the dam to reach the corner of Chew reservoir. Holme Moss transmitter can be seen across the plateau looking eastwards.

2. With your back to the corner of the reservoir, turn sharp right and follow the moorland path away from the reservoir. Follow the ridge on the opposite side of the steep valley to the access road you have just walked up. A sign marking the boundary of open country is soon reached and continue from here along a distinct stony path which follows the edge of the ridge with the crags and deep valley of Chew Brook to the right. If visibility is poor, navigation with map and compass will certainly be required here and for the next few miles of this walk. After crossing a babbling brook it is important to spot a waymarker post and cairn to the left of the path. This shows a yellow arrow and is dedicated to the memory of Walter and Doris Brookfield. Turn sharp left from the ridge path and follow the line (a permissive path) indicated by the waymarker which heads south-west across the moor. There is no distinct path across the peat moor but there a number of waymarker posts which lead across several streams and over the brow of the boggy hill to a stile in a fence line. There is a M.A.F.F. sign on the stile indicating the heather regeneration work in this designated Environmentally Sensitive Area. On a clear day, the view from here is nothing short of spectacular!

3. Cross the stile and take in the view. The highest point of Hoarstone Edge lies less than half a mile away – this is the flat and featureless plateau to your right. The two nearby hills ahead, towards the Man-

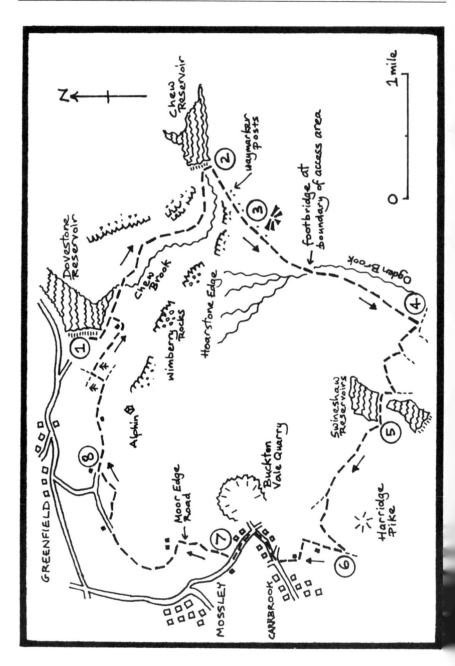

chester conurbation, are Hollingworthall moor (the grassy one on the left) and Harridge Pike (heather moor on the right). Beyond them lies the city, Werneth Low, the Peak District and Cheshire hills. Look north to reveal Windy Hill and the Cliviger wind farms. To continue the walk, go directly ahead from the stile following the long line of waymarker posts, heading downhill in the direction of reservoirs. The route is unclear but the waymarker posts lead down to another stile in a fence. From here, bear slightly left in the direction of the single (Arnfield) reservoir to pick up a distinct path (indicated by cairns) through heather and ferns. The path almost meets a fence coming in from the right across the hillside and drops down to a footbridge over the Ogden Brook alongside another sign marking the boundary of open country. The pleasant path through heather clings to the hillside to the right of the little valley, Ogden Clough and follow this for over half a mile to reach a junction of paths near a wall.

4. Turn sharp right at the waymarker post before the wall facing you is reached and follow the grassy track uphill with the wall to the left. Cross a stile and keep by the wall-side as it turns a corner, swinging left to a latch gate in the wall by another waymarker post. Go through the gate to the other side of the wall and turn sharp right heading towards the line of electricity pylons. These infamous pylons head east up over the Pennines and manage to blight the Longdendale valley. The grass path soon swings left around the hillside to another waymarker post, look straight ahead for a view of Audenshaw Reservoirs on a clear day. At the waymarker post, turn sharp right and go downhill, passing through a kissing gate to join the reservoir access road. Follow the road across the dam between the Higher and Lower Swineshaw Reservoirs. On the far side, another waymarker post is reached at a junction of paths.

5. Take the path signed for 'Carrbrook 2 miles' which leads uphill along a stone track to a nearby wooden shack. The track turns right in front of the shack and then runs uphill as a wide path cut through the heather. Follow this uphill for the next half a mile and the track then starts to drop down over the brow to a reveal a view of Mossley and Hartshead Pike. The moor rising to your left is Harridge Pike but there is no right of way to the summit. Avoid a path forking right but keep left above the valley and the track soon runs alongside a wall, swinging left around the hillside which overlooks the modern residential estates of Carrbrook. The path heads in the direction of

Stalybridge, to the left of which is Harrop Edge (the hill with masts) and look west for an extensive view of Manchester. Cross a stile to reach a waymarker post.

6. Turn right along the track signposted for 'Carrbrook ½ mile' and drop downhill past a cottage on the left. Approximately 100 metres after passing the cottage look out for a gate and stile on the left, cross the stile and follow the waymarked grass path downhill between fences. Go through a gate and turn right in front of the house and walk down the driveway passing under trees to the rear of gardens. At the bottom of the drive a road is reached. Turn right and take the left fork (not South View) to follow a road lined with cottages past Buckton Vale Club (with an 1897 datestone). Follow the continuation of the road, signed as Carr Rise and at the crossroads turn left into Castle Lane. Follow the lane uphill for about a quarter of a mile until a cottage is reached on the left. Leave the lane here by forking right up a rough track to a signpost for 'Chew Valley 2 miles' pointing up a stone road.

7. The path follows this old highway known as Moor Edge Road overlooking Mossley which clings to the hillside above the Tame Valley. The hillside to the right is Buckton Moor which has been severely affected by quarrying. The site of medieval Buckton Castle is marked on the O.S. map above the steep slope but is not visible from the road. Follow the road for the next mile and a quarter, keeping to the main track which swings left after passing cottages and then is met by a private road from the right. At this point, bear left then take the right fork maintaining a level height above the valley. The road eventually swings around the hillside to reveal Wharmton Hill, Greenfield and Pots and Pans. When the lane passes a cluster of cottages on your left, look out for a stile marked with an Oldham Way waymarker (an owl) on the right of the lane, almost opposite the last cottage (Hill Cottage) before the road starts to drop downhill. Leave the road here and cross the stile, continuing directly ahead across the hillside to another stile. The path then swings around a little valley, crossing over another stile and dropping down a track to reach a tarmac farm road.

8. Turn right here and head up the valley towards Dovestone Reservoir. The steep-sided ridge rising on your right is Alphin, the rival of Alderman Hill on the opposite side of the Chew Valley. Follow the

farm road for half a mile until it passes between cottages and look out for a waymarked path (Oldham Way) on the right-hand side next to the cottage. Take this walled track, which keeps above the valley and climbs gradually to a conifer plantation to the right of Dovestone Reservoir. The plantation is joined on the left and a kissing gate is reached. Go through the gate, cross a little brook and almost immediately turn sharp left, leaving the main path through the woodland to descend the hillside along a path between the brook and the conifers. At the bottom edge of the woodland, cross a wall and turn sharp right to walk along the edge of the field with the wall and plantation on your right. There is no distinct path but continue in the same direction for approximately a quarter of a mile, crossing derelict walls and keeping the plantation edge to your right until a kissing gate is reached. Continue straight ahead along the field edge to reach a white gate next to a farmhouse. Go through the gate and follow the farm road downhill to join the reservoir road. Turn left here to retrace your steps to the car park.

15. Hartshead Pike

This walk climbs one of the closest hills to Manchester city centre from the industrial hamlet of Park Bridge, hidden in the upper reaches of the Medlock
Valley.

Peaks and Panoramas: HARTSHEAD PIKE is not a high hill but it forms a
prominent ridge rising steeply from the valley pastures of the River Medlock.
It is easily identifiable by its 19th century round tower and the summit also
has an information board and viewpoint indicator. The Pike offers contrasting
views – westward lies Ashton, Oldham and the city centre and eastward lies
Mossley, Saddleworth and the Peak District hills.

Distance: 4 miles

Map: O.S. Pathfinder 713 Oldham

Start: Park Bridge Heritage Centre car park, Dean Terrace, Park Bridge
(Grid Reference 939 026). Note that the car park closes at 5pm.

Getting there: Park Bridge can be reached from either the A627
Oldham-Ashton Road or the B6194 Lees Road. If approaching from the
A627 turn off at Park Bridge Road by a car showroom and follow the winding
road which is cobbled and suffers from big potholes in places. From the
B6194 turn off at Alt Hill Lane. The Park Bridge Heritage Centre is situated
halfway up a hill next to old mill remains and the car park is directly opposite.

Public transport: There is no direct bus service to Park Bridge but services
between Oldham and Ashton stop by the junction of Abbey Hills Road and Alt
Lane to the north of the hamlet. From here walk down Alt Lane, turning left
into Dean Terrace to arrive at the heritage centre. The return journey will add
approximately 2 miles to the walk length.

Background

The River Medlock rises on hill slopes of Saddleworth in the vicinity of
Grains Bar and flows six miles in a south-west direction to join the River
Irwell at Castlefield, Manchester. This walk starts along its upper middle reaches, where the Medlock's waters gave rise to the 19th century
industrial community of Park Bridge. It was here that Samuel and
Hannah Lees set up an iron works in the 1780s which expanded into a
large family business providing machinery for nearby textile mills.
Rows of houses (Dean and Dingle Terraces), a school and church were
built for the workers in the 1850s and 1860s and the Lees family themselves lived in the Gothic Dean House. A railway line between Ashton

and Oldham once passed through Park Bridge on a viaduct over the river and there was even a village station. There were coal mines and cotton mills in the valley hereabouts and the hamlet enjoyed a Victorian and Edwardian heyday attracting hundreds of workers from the nearby towns. Post-war industrial decline inevitably killed off Park Bridge and the little hamlet has regained its turn off the century atmosphere. In fact, I have often seen a horse and cart clip-clop down the cobbled road to cross the Medlock.

One can only assume that Park Bridge has not been submerged by the sprawl of modern housing estates creeping in from Oldham and Ashton because of the curious topography of the site. At Rocher Vale, the Medlock meanders through a steep-sided gorge that was created by retreating ice sheets at the end of the last Ice Age. Numerous abandoned mines and mine shafts also litter the valley and the walk passes close to the walled remains of the pumping station of an old mine.

The walk climbs to the round brick tower on Hartshead Pike with its distinctive conical roof. The present tower dates from 1863 and was built to celebrate the royal wedding of the Prince of Wales and Princess Alexandra of Denmark. This replaced an 18th century tower and the present structure was itself restored in the 1920s. The Pike itself has

Rocher Vale crossing

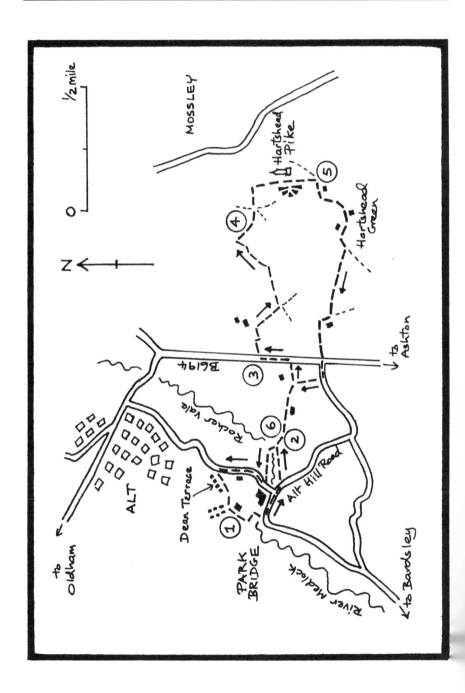

been a beacon site probably since Roman times and certainly since the 16th century when it was an Armada beacon. A fire was lit here to warn of the threat of the Spanish Armada and it linked to a chain of hilltop beacons which included Rivington Pike (visited in Walk 1). Elizabethan Mancunians would probably have spotted the warning fire as Hartshead Pike is only 8 miles away, giving the closest views of the city centre to be found in this book.

The Route

1. From the heritage centre (a former stables) follow the lane downhill to cross over the River Medlock in the valley bottom. Turn left up the road signposted as Alt Hill Road and you soon get a view of Hartshead Pike straight ahead. When the road forks, take the right fork, signposted for Hartshead Pike and soon a track is reached on the left-hand side of the road. Follow this track above a little valley until another waymarker post is reached. Take the path signed for 'Hartshead Pike 1½ miles' which bears right and enters a birch woodland. Keep to the right of a small brook and climb wooden steps to reach a stile at the top of the woodland.

2. Cross the stile, turn left and follow the field edge to another stile in the field corner behind a cottage. There is a good view south-westwards to Manchester from here. Cross this stile and continue alongside the hedge to reach the access road to the cottage (Colts Hey Farm). Continue straight ahead in the direction of the Pike and when the road starts to swing sharp right look out for a waymarked path leading off to the left. Follow this path which crosses a field between fences and brings you out on a busy road (Lees Road) through a squeeze stile. Turn left and follow the road for approximately 150 metres until the access road to a farm on the right-hand side of the road is reached.

3. Turn right and walk up the access road towards the stone farm. Before reaching it, look for a waymarker post on your right. Turn right and follow the path across the grass to the fence line, then turn left and continue up the hill to a nearby stile. Cross the stile and follow the field edge, with the fence on your right to reach a junction of paths in the opposite field corner. Turn left and follow the path signed for Hartshead Pike, which leads uphill along the fence line.

Ahead of you is a pleasant rural view, behind you are the urban grandeurs of Failsworth, Droylsden and the city centre. The path soon drops downhill to a spring and squeeze stile. Continue uphill towards a cottage, then bear left to another waymarker post. Continue along the path signposted for Hartshead Pike, which keeps the fence to your right and reaches a stile in the corner of a stone wall. Cross the stile and continue in the same direction along a rough track closely following the line of a disused wall. The path heads in the direction of the nearby Oldham golf course, but look out for a sudden change of direction indicated by a waymarker post. The path swings sharp right near a holly bush and climbs steeply up the hillside to a stile.

4. Cross the stile and at this junction of paths take the most direct route uphill, crossing the access road and crossing another stile to follow the path leading directly to the Pike between a wall and fence. Go through the gap in the wall at the top of the hill and turn right to follow the track to the Pike. The present tower is Victorian and its history is outlined on an information panel. The viewpoint indicator highlights the Welsh Hills (78 miles away!) but much nearer features to be seen include Tandle Hill, Werneth Low, the Chew Valley (in a gorge of jagged rocks) and Buckton Quarry, whilst Ashton and Oldham are the nearby towns. To continue the walk, follow the ridge downhill from the viewpoint indicator to reach a rough access road.

5. Turn right and follow this road downhill past cottages and derelict farm buildings. The road soon becomes wide and tarmacked. Approximately 250 metres after passing Hartshead Hall, look for a waymarked path for Lees Road which forks off the road on the right. The path leads through a gate and follows a wide track between fences. Cross two fields before reaching the access road again, opposite a cottage. Join the road via a stile, a few metres to the right of a gate. Turn right and follow the road as it swings left and soon reaches a road junction. Go directly across the junction by following Alt Hill Lane for approximately 60 metres before turning right down a farm access road. Follow this as it swings around to the point where you left it earlier. Retrace your steps for the next quarter of a mile by following the path alongside the hedge of Colts Hey Farm, along the field edge and over the stile and down the steps to the waymarker post on the edge of the birch woodland.

6. Do not retrace your steps along the track from here. Instead, turn right and head towards the nearby wooden bridge which crosses the river Medlock. The ruined building nearby is an old mine pump house, a legacy of Victorian industry. The gorge-like valley looking upstream is known hereabouts as Rocher Vale. Cross the wooden bridge and follow the track lined with railway sleepers through the heather and scrub keeping the babbling Medlock on your left. A lane is soon joined, with a factory with a blue roof directly opposite. Turn right and follow the lane uphill for nearly a quarter of a mile until Dean Terrace is reached on the left. Turn into Dean Terrace and follow this downhill past the site of Park Bridge's church and school, Dean House and an interesting row of workers' cottages along Dingle Terrace. The visitor centre and car park are then reached.

16. Hollingworthall Moor

This walk climbs up past the reservoirs of the Brushes Valley on the edge of Stalybridge and ascends the prominent moorland mass of Hollingworthall Moor overlooking the town. The route crosses the ridge of the moor and descends to woodland around Hollingworth Hall before climbing back up to the summit triangulation pillar. An alternative route is also suggested which takes a shorter, more direct approach to the summit. This does not follow a definitive right of way but is well-used by the public and traverses land owned by North West Water. The advantage of the alternative route is that it keeps to the higher part of the ridge but does mean a slightly shorter route – the total mileage of the walk following the alternative section to the summit is 6 miles. Both routes take in the summit of Hollingworthall Moor from where there is a steep and quick descent back to the Brushes Valley. It also links with Walk 14 (Hoarstone Edge) giving an opportunity for a longer walk.

Peaks and Panoramas: HOLLINGWORTHALL MOOR dominates the walk just as it dominates the town of Stalybridge below it. An oddly-contoured mass of rough pasture, its northern slopes are more wild as deep cloughs cut into it and streams run steeply down to the Brushes Reservoirs. Its southern slopes are more gentle and its pastures roll down into Longdendale. The views from the moor are exceptional in all directions and from the triangulation pillar looking west, the whole of Greater Manchester lies close at hand. It is a good spot to examine the geography of the Pennine edges as Hollingworthall Moor appears as one of a long line of escarpments which include Werneth Low, Harrop Edge, Harridge Pike and Buckton Moor. Views north look to Saddleworth and south and east to Cown Edge, Glossop, Longdendale and the Peak District.

Distance: 7 miles

Map: Ordnance Survey Outdoor Leisure Sheet 1 The Peak District (Dark Peak Area)

Start: Stalybridge Country Park, Oakgates Visitor Centre car park, Hartley Street, off Huddersfield Road, Millbrook, Stalybridge (Grid Reference 979 994)

Getting there: Stalybridge Country Park is signposted along the B6175 Huddersfield Road which runs between Stalybridge and Mossley. The car park entrance is about a mile north-west of Stalybridge town centre by a bend in the road at Millbrook and adjacent to the Royal Oak pub car park. Turn right by the Royal Oak if approaching from Stalybridge. The car park is just on the left immediately after turning; if there is no space available it may be possible to park on Grove Road, the lane on the opposite side of Huddersfield Road.

Public transport: Numerous bus services between Manchester, Ashton and Mossley stop along Huddersfield at Millbrook. Alight by the Royal Oak.

Background

It is worth enduring the first five minutes of this walk which encounters the urban fringe countryside overlooking the Brushes council estate. For almost immediately the town is left behind and the Brushes valley, with its four reservoirs, provides a gateway to wild moorland on the edge of the Peak District. Hollingworthall Moor is an untamed clump of water authority moorland that acts as an important buffer to industrial Stalybridge. The transition to pleasant countryside is so swift that, amazingly, the Peak District National Park begins less than two and a half miles from the council houses that back on to the Brushes Valley. The newly developed Stalybridge Country Park is a noble attempt to improve the local environment in the much abused section of valley below the reservoirs and it has at least saved it from being turned into a refuse tip.

The Swineshaw Brook descends from the boggy plateau of Hoarstone Edge and forms the catchment for the Higher and Lower Swineshaw, Brushes and Walkerwood reservoirs before flowing down to the River Tame beyond Millbrook. Pre-1974 the county boundary between Lancashire and Cheshire passed through the three upper reservoirs with Cheshire lying on the south side of the valley. The reservoirs, a quarry railway and the electricity pylons which continue east up Longdendale have all had an impact on the valley which manages to remain pleasant to look at thanks to the wild northern slopes of Hollingworthall Moor. The southern slopes of the moor present a more pastoral face, rolling down to the site of Hollingworth Hall and Hollingworth village at the gateway to Longdendale.

Standing on the summit of Hollingworthall Moor is perhaps the best way to gain an understanding of the geography of the Manchester region for it is one of a

The summit above the city

line of Pennine foot hills with steep western slopes that rise above a plain cloaked in urban and industrial sprawl. The hard rocks of the Pennine uplift end here and the Manchester Basin, begins - a vast lowland covered by glacial till which has become an ideal natural site for the development of a metropolis.

Incidentally, on different Ordnance Survey maps Hollingworthall Moor is often spelt as Hollingworthhall Moor. I have dropped my 'h', so to speak, just to save on typing.

The Route

1. Walk up from the car park and pass through the kissing gate by the Oakgates Visitor Centre – an uninviting brown shack – and continue straight ahead to the right of the Centre along the path waymarked for 'Walkerwood Reservoir ½ mile'. This path leads uphill through woodland and bears right to emerge alongside the back of council houses. Do not turn off to the left along any side tracks but follow the path at the rear of the estate to arrive at a pedestrian access that leads out onto a lane, Brushes Road. Turn left on the lane and follow it for a short distance until a step in the stone wall and waymarker signpost is reached on the right of the lane. Leave the lane here and cross over the wall to follow the path, signed 'Brushes Road via Cock Wood 2/3 mile'. This distinct path runs parallel to the lane heading up the valley and crosses a stile before running through scrub and descending into a woodland. Walkerwood Reservoir can be seen below and the steep slopes of Harridge Pike (north side) and Hollingworthall Moor (south side) rise on either side of the valley. The path bears left and runs downhill along the fence of a conifer plantation to reach a gate and stile at the top end of the reservoir.

2. Cross the stile and turn left along the track between the Walkerwood and Brushes Reservoirs. This swings around to go through another gate and climb uphill between two walls to reach a crossroads of routes. Turn sharp right and go through another gate, following the tarmac access road, Brushes Road, up the valley. This road meanders uphill above the reservoirs for the next mile until it reaches the embankment of the Higher Swineshaw Reservoir. It provides a good view down the valley to Ashton and the city centre and right to the back end of Hollingworthall Moor. The embankment between the Higher and Lower Swineshaw Reservoirs is eventually reached by a

waymarker post and to the north lies the brooding plateau of Hoarstone Edge. Turn right and cross the dam along the footpath waymarked for Hollingworth Hall Farm. Go through the gate on the far side of the dam then take the path forking right which leads through a kissing gate and passes under pylons to reach a waymarker signpost by a tree.

3. Turn right and take the path signposted for 'Hollingworth Hall Farm 1¼ miles'. This bears left along a distinct track with a wall to the right of it. The track climbs gradually and Ashton and Manchester again come into view, whilst Harridge Pike can be identified on the north side of the valley as it has several rectangular strips of heather removed from its slopes. The wall ends and the track peters out slightly amongst rushes, but just continue in the same direction and look out for a wooden stile and waymarker signpost in the wall ahead. Continue uphill through the next field to reach another stile at the far wall boundary. From here, head diagonally left uphill to a waymarker post in the wall boundary on the left, alongside a ladder stile and gate. There is a choice of routes: either continue uphill along the inviting ridge to the summit of Hollingworthall Moor or cross the ladder stile and take a slightly longer walk to the summit, following a route which has good views east to the Peak District. The alternative route is highlighted in Paragraph 5 below.

4. For the longer route, cross the ladder stile and follow the field edge down to another stile and gate. The view from here includes Arnfield Reservoir, Dinting Viaduct, Longdendale, Coombes Edge and Werneth Low. Cross the stile and bear diagonally right along a track which leads downhill towards a woodland. At the bottom corner of the field another track is reached at a waymarker signpost. Turn right along this track following the path waymarked for Hollingworth Hall Farm which crosses a stile by a gate and shortly passes the farm buildings. Continue straight ahead along the track through the farm entrance and it passes a number of cottages and becomes a tarmac lane. Follow the lane with excellent views for approximately half a mile as it swings right then left and then reaches overhead pylons by a footpath sign on the right. Leave the lane here along the path which crosses a stile by a gate then leads uphill along a stony track running alongside a fence then a wall to the right. The track runs uphill to face a wall and turns sharp left, heading back towards the line of pylons. Cross a stile by a gate and follow the wide

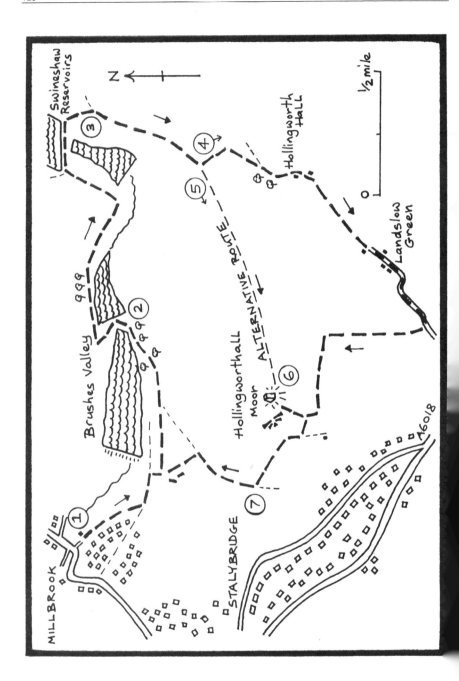

path cut through the heather which leads under the pylons to a cairn at a crossroads of paths. Turn right on the track here and continue uphill to shortly reach the summit pillar of Hollingworthall Moor.

5. For the shorter route to the summit do not cross over the ladder stile in the wall but follow the ridge uphill to a gate by a line of telegraph poles, keeping the wall on the left. Go through the gate and the path becomes more distinct, follow it uphill through rough pasture as it bears slightly left and the view opens out on both sides of the ridge. The plateau levels out then starts to climb again, crossing stiles and heads towards a prominent square sign (an old water authority sign) which stands on the brow of the hill directly ahead. Aim for the sign and cross the stile in the derelict wall close by and a narrow path in the heather then meanders around to the summit pillar. The breathtaking view over the edge will take you by surprise. The sprawling Manchester metropolis is laid out below and easy to spot are Stalybridge, Ashton, Oldham, Audenshaw Reservoirs and the city centre, just over nine miles away directly east. In fact, a straight line can be drawn on the map between the summit pillar and Manchester Town Hall. Looking south, Harrop Edge is the little hill of cluttered masts and pylons which overlooks Hattersley and beyond this is the Idle Hill-Werneth Low ridge. Looking north, Harridge Pike is the next hill along and beyond this Buckton Moor with Hartshead Pike on the opposite side of the Tame Valley.

6. From the summit head southwards in the direction of Harrop Edge, following the track back down to the cairn and crossroads of paths under the line of pylons. Turn right here and drop down the hillside towards a line of telegraph poles to reach a stile in a wall/fence. Follow the path through the grass which leads diagonally downhill to a track at a stile and gate. Turn right on this grass track, signposted for 'Brushes ¾ mile' but, after approximately 100 metres, look for a waymarker post on the left indicating a path, joined by crossing over the step-stile in the wall. Follow this path diagonally downhill through rough pasture, it runs between the lines of pylons and telegraph poles which are unwelcome companions and cannot be shaken off. The path then meets another track, running left to right, by a waymarker post.

7. Turn right and follow this track, which maintains the same height and skirts around the hillside. Head in the direction of Walkerwood

Reservoir and follow the path for about quarter of a mile mile without dropping down the hill until you have passed the disused brick rifle ranges which can be seen below. Then turn left and go steeply downhill along a faint path through the heather to reach a stone track at the corner of the rifle ranges. Turn left and pass the disused buildings to reach a waymarked stile in a wire fence on the right. Cross this and drop steeply down to the waymarker post and step-stile in the wall passed earlier on the walk. Retrace your steps back to the car park by turning left along Brushes Road and following it for a short distance until you reach the Stalybridge Country Park sign on the right. Turn right here and go down the path back to the visitor centre and car park.

17. Werneth Low

This walk descends to the Etherow Valley at Compstall then climbs steeply to the greens of Werneth Low golf course, before traversing the well-trodden moorland ridge from Idle Hill to the Werneth Low War Memorial.

Peaks and Panoramas: WERNETH LOW ridge has a triangulation pillar at its south-western end but reaches its highest point at IDLE HILL, at the opposite end of the gently rising plateau. Masts of a transmitter station occupy this higher ground and on the road side below them is a viewpoint indicator looking east to Longdendale and the Peak District. Werneth Low is easily identifiable by the tall War Memorial erected to the people of Hyde. There is also a viewpoint indicator close to the Cenotaph revealing extensive views west and north to Manchester, Stockport and the Tameside towns, Hollingworthall Moor and Saddleworth.

Distance: 4½ miles

Map: Ordnance Survey Outdoor Leisure Sheet 1: The Peak District (Dark Peak Area)

Start: Werneth Low Country Park car park, Werneth Low Road, Gee Cross (Grid Reference 960 928)

Getting there: Werneth Low Country Park is signposted from the A560 Stockport Road/Mottram Old Road, but note that the starting point is not the lower car park which is for the Lower Higham Visitor Centre on Higham Lane. The Werneth Low Road car park is higher up the hill than this, adjacent to a minor crossroads and phone box.

Public transport: A very limited service between Marple, Hyde and High Lane stops on Werneth Low Road. However, there are plenty of buses which stop at Gee Cross with numerous services running between Manchester, Hyde, Romiley and Marple. Alight on Stockport Road and walk up Joel Lane at the top of which is the Werneth Low country park car park. The return journey from Gee Cross to the start of the walk should only add about a mile to the walk route.

Background

The sentinel-like ridge of Werneth Low, rising to a height of 900 feet (273 metres), stands guard against the urban sprawl of Tameside and Stockport, an outlying hill at the western edge of the higher Peak District edges. It forms a natural barrier to development, preventing Hyde and Romiley merging into one and keeps the grim tower blocks of post-war Hattersley at bay, thus protecting the pleasant patchwork of pastures and woodland which makes up the fair face of the Etherow Valley. The highest point of Werneth Low ridge, which roughly runs in a north-east – south-west direction, is Idle Hill, at the north-eastern end where radio masts now stand. From here, there are excellent views of the two natural gateways into Derbyshire formed by the Rivers Etherow and Goyt. It is not surprising that An-

glo-Saxon settlers were attracted to the ridge and that they buried their dead in barrows here.

Upon this urban fringe country-side have developed two country parks: at Werneth Low (with a visitor centre at Lower Higham) and the Etherow Valley (with a visitor centre at Compstall). The former is con-trolled by Tameside Metropolitan Borough and the latter by Stockport Metropolitan Borough as the bound-ary between the two actually passes over Werneth Low and cuts the hill in half, administratively speaking. Most of the Werneth Low Country Park is owned by the Hyde War Me-morial Trust and the monument re-membering the town's dead from the Great War was erected in 1920.

The River Etherow at Compstall has been a popular beauty spot for years and the village grew up around

Hyde's war memorial

the 1820s cotton mill of entrepreneur George Andrew. A village pub (passed on the walk) bears his name and his estate stretched up the wooded valley which now forms the country park. In stark contrast to this Victorian village is the modern 'village' of Hattersley, the starkness of which is clearly in view from the northern face of Werneth Low. Hattersley was an attempt to solve Manchester's inner city housing problem by creating new self-contained overspill estates in the pleasant countryside on the edge of the city. I think it must have been the brain-child of a council planner who lived in Wilmslow. Luckily, this walk only has to view Hattersley from a very comfortable distance.

The Route

1. From the car park turn left and walk to the crossroads alongside the 'phone box. Turn left after the 'phone box and join the track signed as Mount Road. There is also a footpath signpost here indicating the way to Compstall and Broadbottom. The track very quickly forks – take the right fork which passes a cricket ground on your right. When the track starts to swing around to the right towards a cottage, continue straight ahead, dropping downhill along a grass path, fenced on either side. The path drops down to a gate in a wall next to a hidden cottage aptly named Grand View. There are excellent views looking south from here to the luxuriant woodland of the nearby Etherow Valley and beyond to Furness Vale – a gateway to the Peak District. Go through the wooden gate and continue straight ahead, dropping down through the field to reach another wooden gate close to some trees and a telegraph pole.

2. Do not go through this gate but turn sharp right along the access track and follow this as it runs behind farm buildings to reach a field gate. Go through this gate and follow the grassy path alongside a tree-lined hedge. Follow this path for nearly half a mile, passing through a gateway, until it reaches a waymarked stile and gateway to the left of farm buildings. Cross the stile and turn right to pass through a gate and reach the farm buildings. Continue straight ahead between the farm buildings to reach a gate on the left behind them. The path heads south through a field and skirts along the top of a wooded valley on your right. Go through the next field and drop downhill keeping above the woodland. Under pylons the path crosses a stream and climbs up to a stile. Cross this and climb the steps to reach a road (the B6104 from Bredbury to Marple Bridge). Turn left and follow the pavement downhill for nearly a quarter of a mile, to arrive in Compstall village.

3. After passing a church entrance on your left, turn left up George Street and walk past the village post office and social club. On the right-hand side of the road is the car park entrance to the Etherow Country Park cafe and visitor centre. Continue along George Street and keep to the main village street as it swings to the left of a row of cottages and climbs uphill past the Andrew Arms and the Methodist church. The road is then signed as School Lane – follow this steeply

uphill for about half a mile, leaving the village behind and passing School Lane Farm and Campville Farm. Approximately 80 metres after passing Campville Farm, the lane swings sharp left. At this point, leave the lane by turning right and follow the path between a hedge and a wooden fence down to a stile in a field corner. Cross the stile and follow the field-edge path downhill to steps and a culvert. Climb steps on the far side of the culvert and follow the faint path uphill through the field to reach a signpost and stile at the top of the field, close to electricity pylons.

4. Cross the stile and turn right on the tarmac farm road. There are good views back towards Furness Vale. Keep to the farm road, passing through the white gates of Beacom Cottages and then northwards under pylons, passing Werneth Low golf course on your left. The nearby peaks of Mottram Hill, Harrop Edge and Hollingworthhall Moor can be seen, together with the villages of Broadbottom and Hadfield. They are backed by the higher hills of the Dark Peak. The farm road eventually swings sharp left and climbs uphill as a tarmac road passing radio masts on your right, before reaching the junction with a lane. You are now closest to the summit of Idle Hill, which lies just to the right, in the enclosed field with the radio masts.

5. Cross the lane and go through the gap in the wall, turning right to follow the path adjacent to the lane between the wall and a wire fence. The delightful tower blocks of Hattersley lie ahead of you! Follow the path down to the nearby buildings at Windy Harbour. In the car park on the far side of the buildings stands a viewpoint indicator on a plinth. From here, Manchester city centre and Kinder Scout can be viewed in opposite directions. The actual route continues by turning left before the buildings at Windy Harbour and going through a pedestrian access, close to a display board for Werneth Low Country Park. Follow the distinct path, signposted for the Cenotaph. The path follows the ridge for nearly half a mile to reach the imposing monument, the War Memorial to the people of Hyde. Another viewpoint indicator stands close by, highlighting such sights as Manchester Airport, Reddish Vale viaduct and Stockport. Manchester and all the towns east of the city can be viewed from here, in stark contrast to the verdant vale of the Etherow and the Peak District edges which were viewed on the south side of the hill.

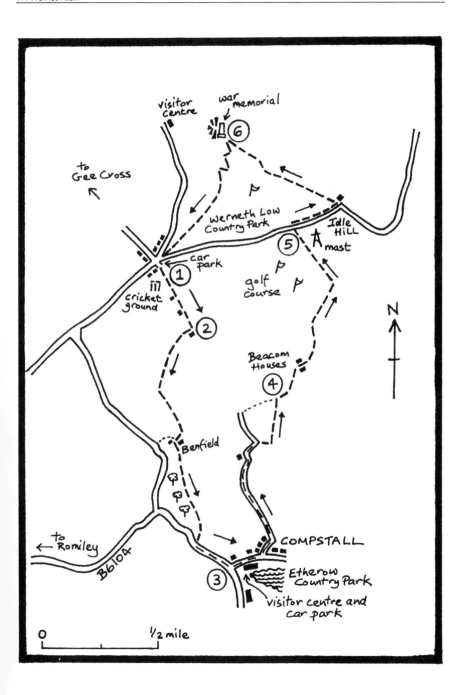

6. From the War Memorial, look back towards the golf course and take the path which forks right, heading for a gap in a stone wall. Go through the gap and keep the wall on your right, following the edge of the golf course. The wall quickly changes direction. Turn right and follow the well-made path alongside the wall. Turn left and keep to the wall-side, heading in a south-westerly direction away from the War Memorial. After nearly half a mile, Werneth Low Road is reached beyond two gates, a picnic area and a display board. The car park is on the far side of the road.

18. Cown Edge and Coombes Rocks

This walk starts in a secluded valley hamlet on the edge of Derbyshire and traverses open moorland before climbing to the prominent ridge of Cown Edge and Coombes Edge. It descends the ridge, passes the remains of two ancient crosses and follows field paths and farm tracks back to picturesque Rowarth. Almost all the walk lies in Derbyshire and within the boundary of the Peak District National Park.

Peaks and Panoramas: The elongated ridge of COWN EDGE dominates the skyline and offers a majestic welcome to the uplands of the Derbyshire Peak District. It rises quite gently north of Rowarth but becomes decidedly more dramatic at its northern end where it merges into the steep sided western face of the bowl-like COOMBES EDGE. At this point, rock outcrops are found on both sides of the thin-topped ridge. Cown Edge Rocks, affected by quarrying, look east to panoramic views across the Kinder plateau. Coombes Edge Rocks, affected by dramatic landslips, look west towards the eastern side of Greater Manchester.

Distance: 7 miles

Map: Ordnance Survey Outdoor Leisure Sheet 1 The Peak District (Dark Peak Area)

Start: Rowarth public car park, off Hollinsmoor Road, Rowarth, Derbyshire (Grid Reference 012 892)

Getting there: Rowarth lies at a dead end of minor roads and can be approached either from Mellor by turning left along Shiloh Road or Charlesworth by turning left down Gun Road and look out for a minor crossroads close to the Moorfield Arms. At this crossroads, turn downhill along Hollinsmoor Road and after about half a mile look for a lane on the left, signed for Rowarth only. The lane leads uphill to a car park on the right by a post box.

There is alternative parking in the valley bottom at Rowarth close to the Little Mill Inn. This is reached by continuing down the hill and not turning off left for Rowarth only.

Public transport: There is a very limited bus service from Marple, Marple Bridge and Mill Brow which stops at Rowarth car park. But this only runs a couple of days a week.

It is hard to believe that this exhilarating Peak District walk lies just over ten miles from Manchester city centre, particularly as the top of Cown Edge feels just a stone's throw away from the peat plateau of Kinder Scout, the boggy guardian of the Dark Peak. The gritstone edge of Cown Rocks is a prelude to the high ridges of the Peak District to the east but, looking west from here, the moorland descends to the lush Etherow Valley and only rises once more to the west of the Etherow in the gentler form of Werneth Low. After Werneth Low, we suddenly hit Hyde, Denton, Gorton and the city centre.

The swirling topography around Rowarth is dominated by a succession of scarp slopes and valleys. Erosional forces, including the ice sheets which once passed through here, carved out valleys in softer shale rocks to leave prominent 'edges' of more resistant sandstone. The shear sandstone cliff of Coombes Edge has been formed as a result of a succession of landslides which have caused severe slumping here and the earliest landslides occurred several thousand years ago.

Nestling below the southern slopes of Cown Edge is the valley hamlet of Rowarth, a hidden nook of Derbyshire with 18th and 19th century houses which prospered on the back of the old water mill in the valley bottom, now an interesting inn. Of more ancient origin are the remains of two Anglo-Saxon crosses, passed on the walk below Coombes Rocks. The dual crosses, two of several found on the borders of Cheshire and Derbyshire, were probably vandalised by Puritans but are curiously marked on the map as Robin Hood's Picking Rods. Robin Hood (see also Robin Hood's Bed in Walk 9), a popular mythological figure in the north, always manages to pop up to describe curious topographical fea-

Robin Hood's Picking Rods – ancient cross shafts?

ures. One suggestion for the 'picking rods' tag is that local men would
)ick their wives at this spot!

The picking rods have always been an important boundary marker.
[he old parishes of Rowarth, Chisworth, Mellor and Ludworth met
1ere and it marks the county boundary between Cheshire (now Greater
√Ianchester) and Derbyshire. The same boundary is also the boundary
)f the Peak District National Park.

The Route

I. Turn right on leaving the car park and walk towards the cottages
   which make up the hamlet of Rowarth. When they are reached, take
   the access-only lane leading off to the right past a cottage with a 1797
   datestone. The lane leads down past a 'phone box and ends by an
   1824 datestone in a wall on the right, recording the site of a village
   Sunday School. Do not follow the private drive to the nearby house
   but continue along the bridleway between a wall and fence. The
   bridleway goes through a gap in the wall by the house and continues
   downhill as a stony track, passing other cottages to emerge on a quiet
   lane at the bottom of a hill. Turn left on the lane and pass the unexpected Little Mill Inn with its impressive waterwheel. Save this hostelry for the end of the walk as its far too early to imbibe. Continue
   past the inn, along a lane which swings left and climbs gradually uphill for a short distance before forking into two.

2. Take the right fork and follow the track around the side of a farm on
   the right. The stony track climbs uphill as a sunken route and soon
   gives views looking north to the ridge of Cown Edge, the objective of
   this walk. After about a third of a mile the track changes direction,
   swinging sharp right and heading southwards. Walk uphill in this
   direction for about 100 metres until a metal gate is reached on the
   right-hand side of the track. Opposite the gate, almost turn back on
   yourself to join an unsigned track on the left. Follow this walled
   green lane which overlooks Rowarth in the valley below and it soon
   passes through a gate to reveal views of the high western edges of
   Kinder Scout including the Knott and Mill Hill. The track drops
   down from the gate to reach a waymarker signpost at a junction of
   paths – six paths radiate out from this busy wall corner!

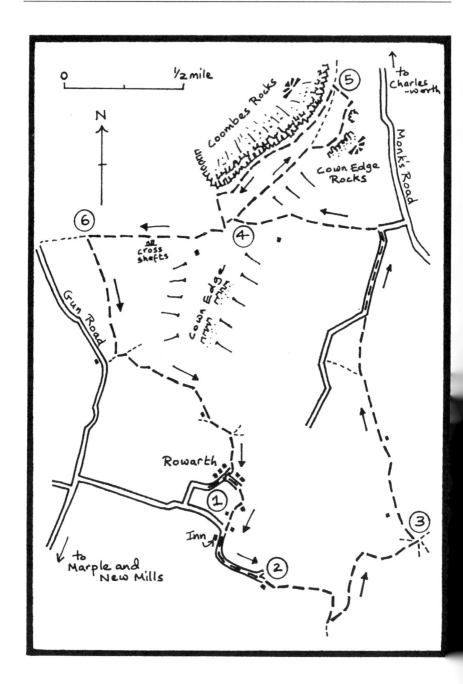

3. Turn left and go through the latch gate to follow the route signed for Monk's Road via Matley Moor. The walk now follows a farm track for over half a mile and heads north towards Cown Edge. When you reach a second farmhouse, bear left around trees to avoid the farmhouse and the wide track continues heading north. Go through a bridle gate and soon the track reaches another gate and stile, after which the track swings left and runs downhill. Cross the stile but leave the track here by continuing straight ahead through a squeeze stile in the wall, on the far side of the track. The path follows a narrow grassy path through heather which heads towards the rock outcrops at the northern end of Cown Edge and runs diagonally up the slope to wooden shacks by a stile in the wall. You are now on the slopes of Matley Moor and there are good views south towards Mellor Moor and Park Moor. Cross the stile and continue straight ahead along the lane, which drops downhill. When the lane swings sharp right, turn sharp left and go through the gate signed for Cown Edge Farm. Follow the farm road uphill for about half a mile. It becomes a stony track and the brow of Cown Edge is reached alongside stiles on either side of the track.

4. From Kinder in the east, the view opens out west to Manchester. The gentle ridge of Werneth Low can be seen rising above Hattersley's tower blocks and the view may also include Oldham and the Peel Tower in the West Pennines. Turn right and cross the stile which leads on to a gently rising plateau. The top of Cown Edge is at its widest here and the path runs across rough pasture to cross another stile by a plantation. One path leads straight ahead from here and another path bears right and runs around the top of Cown Edge Rocks, at their most impressive here. Take the latter path and follow the edge of the ridge to the top of a disused quarry. Keep above the old workings and drop down to a sunken track below a fence. Turn sharp left along the track and head back across the ridge to reach another stile overlooking the western edge. Cross the stile facing you and admire the view. You are on Coombes Edge with Coombes Rocks dramatically slipping away below you. To the right, Coombes Edge winds down to Charlesworth village and also looking north can be seen the Dinting Vale railway viaduct, Harrop Edge and Hollingworthhall Moor above Stalybridge, though nearby Glossop is almost hidden from view.

5. Turn left and follow the well-used path along the top of Coombes Rocks, keeping between the plantation on the left and the shear drop on the right. Cross a stile at the far corner of the plantation and continue along the fence line. Do not follow the edge all the way down hill but, when it starts to descend and swing right, look out for the point when the fence on the left changes direction and turn left here, following the fence line to a nearby stile. Cross the stile and follow the field edge uphill to cross another stile. Continue straight ahead along the track between a wall and fence and this almost immediately turns sharp right and runs downhill to a bridle gate. From the gate, continue straight ahead along the track to reach another gate close to which is a curious stone artefact that resembles a double-funnelled boat. This is in fact the base and shafts of the two ancient crosses marked on the map as Robin Hood's Picking Rods. The gate also marks the boundary of the Peak District National Park and the county boundary between Derbyshire and Greater Manchester. Go through the gate and follow the track along the edge of a large field for about 300 metres until a footpath signpost and stile are reached on the left.

6. Cross the stile over the wall and go diagonally across the field along a faint path to a gate and stile at the next field boundary. Cross the stile and continue in the same direction, heading diagonally across the field to a wall corner. Cross the step-stile over the wall and keep the wall close by on the left and follow the field edge towards a farmhouse. Cross the stile by a signpost on the far side of the field and turn left along a farm track. Almost immediately take the track forking right and then the right fork again to follow a stone track heading for farm buildings further along the hillside. After nearly half a mile the farm, Ayton Farm, is passed on the right and the grass track climbs uphill to a gate and stile. Continue straight ahead, keeping the wall on the immediate right. After a short distance, a waymarker signpost is reached by a stile in the wall. Turn right and cross the stile, following the route signposted for Rowarth. The distinct path crosses three stiles over field boundaries before meeting a lane between houses. Turn right on the lane and continue straight ahead past the cottages to reach the car park on the left.

19. Mellor Moor

This walk descends from Marple Ridge and crosses canal, railway, road and the River Goyt to climb to Mellor Moor on the eastern side of the valley beyond the fairways of Mellor golf course. The route then descends through pastures into Derbyshire and the valley bottom at Strines before following the Peak Forest Canal back to the ridge on the western side of the River Goyt.

Peaks and Panoramas: The wooded MARPLE RIDGE and MELLOR MOOR, both affected by past quarrying activity, face each other on either side of the deep, meandering Goyt Valley. Marple Ridge is traversed by a residential road and has a small car park in an old quarry which provides good views over to Mellor Moor. Mellor Moor is dwarfed by neighbouring Peak District hills but nonetheless it provides magnificent views particularly from COBDEN EDGE on the north side of the moor. The view stretches east to the Kinder plateau and most notably north and west across Marple, Stockport, Manchester and the Cheshire Plain. Mellor Moor has a triangulation pillar, inaccessible by right of way, and a tall cross erected by local churches in the western face of the old quarry.

Distance: 8 miles

Map: Ordnance Survey Outdoor Leisure Sheet 1 The Peak District (Dark Peak Area)

Start: Ridge Quarry viewpoint car park, Ridge Road, Marple (Grid Reference 964 867)

Getting there: The Ridge Quarry car park is about a mile south of Marple on a minor road leading to High Lane and Disley. If approaching from the Stockport end of the A626 turn right at its junction with the B6101 in Marple town centre. The junction has a large garage on the right and the road required, Church Lane, is signposted for All Saint's Church. Church Lane leads uphill past the church, a Conservative Club and the Ring o'Bells pub and continues as Ridge Road. Follow the road past houses until the signed entrance to the car park is reached on the left.

Public transport: A bus service between Marple and High Lane stops on the Ridge Road but this is a limited service. Alternatively, there are train stations at both Marple and Marple Bridge approximately 2 miles form the start of the walk. If starting from Marple Bridge the walk can commence along the Peak Forest Canal above the station. Follow it south for approximately three-quarters of a mile to pick up the walk route at canal bridge number 19 (see the end of instruction 1 in the route directions).

Background

The meandering River Goyt, a main tributary of the River Mersey, flows through Marple Bridge from its source in the Derbyshire hills near Buxton and forms the central feature of this walk which traverses the high slopes on either side of the south-north flowing valley. The Goyt provided a natural corridor for later road, rail and canal developments from urban Manchester to Derbyshire though engineering feats were required to carry both the 1790s Peak Forest Canal and the 1860s Manchester, Sheffield and Lincolnshire Railway through the valley.

The modern history of every northern industrial town begins with a wealthy entrepreneur and Marple was no different. The man in question was Samuel Oldknow, coal and cotton magnate, who invested in the Peak Forest Canal scheme with the intention of bringing limestone from the Peak District to limekilns at Marple. The whole canal, from Ashton to Bugsworth and Whaley Bridge, where it linked with tram roads to limestone quarries was opened in 1800 and enjoyed a busy trade in limestone and coal until the arrival of the railways. Oldknow built the six-storey Mellor Mill on the River Goyt in 1790 and for more than a century it was a major employer in Marple before it burnt down in 1892. The mill ponds survive as the Roman Lakes, though they are not Roman. This tag was only added in late Victorian times by an entrepreneur who tried to turn them into a popular tourist attraction. The romantic idea worked and the Lakes became popular for day trips in Edwardian times, and remain so today.

The pretty octagonal cottage passed under the railway viaduct a bit further along from the Lakes is known as Floodgates Cottage and even this opened as a place of refreshment in Edwardian days. It was originally designed as a toll booth on a proposed turnpike route that subsequently took a different route between New Mills and Marple.

The canal and the countryside around the River Goyt are now used largely for leisure. You are never far away from a golf course in Cheshire (two are passed on this walk) and the riverside paths have been dusted down, knocked into shape and waymarked as the Goyt Way. This 10-mile recreational route follows the river from Whaley Bridge to Compstall, where the Goyt joins the River Etherow. The Peak and Northern Footpaths Preservation Society is active around these parts and their fine green signposts highlight many an old route, including those around the Mellor and Townscliffe golf course. Just remember that the paths were there long before the golfers and recall the words of Mark Twain who once famously remarked that playing golf was a good walk spoilt!

Derbyshire panorama from Mellor Moor

The Route

1. The Ridge Quarry car park gives an excellent view east to Mellor Moor, the objective of this walk. Go out of the car park entrance and turn right, following the lane for a short distance until cottages are reached on the right. Look for the footpath sign between the houses and follow this path through a gap in the wall down to a stile. Walk straight down the hill, keeping a wall on the left and thick gorse on the right. At the corner of the wall, cross over a stile and continue downhill, keeping a fence to the right. The steep path almost disappears under heather but keep going straight ahead to enter the edge of woodland. Go down steps to join a path alongside the Peak Forest Canal. Turn right and cross the bridge (number 21), then sharp left on the far side of the bridge to join the canal towpath. The pleasant towpath is followed in this direction for the next three-quarters of a mile. Stop at the second bridge from here (number 19) which overlooks a road. The towpath continues to Marple Bridge but leave it here by turning right and follow the steps (signed as the Goyt Way) down to the Marple-New Mills road.

2. Cross the road and continue directly ahead along the path opposite,

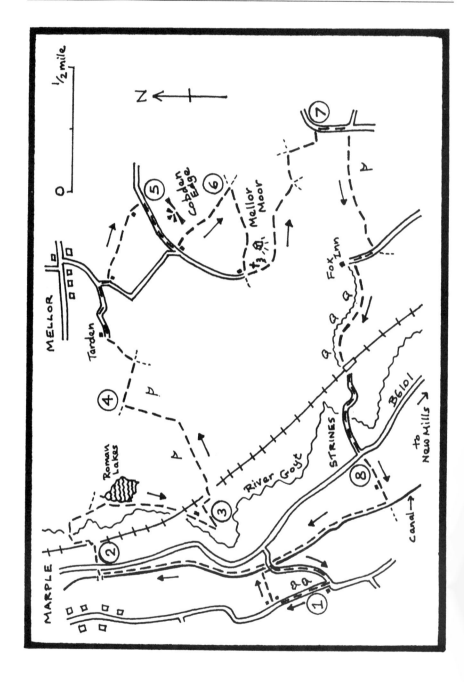

signed as the Goyt Way. This leads downhill between garden hedges, turns sharp left around a railway fence and crosses the bridge over the commuter line from Manchester to Derbyshire. Go down the steps on the far side of the bridge. The path runs parallel to the high railway before dropping down to a wide stone track signed as a private road. Swing right along the track across the wooded River Goyt and, when the track forks, take the right fork, Lakes Road, signed for the Roman Lakes. Follow this for about 250 metres until it forks again with a track veering off to the right. Take this track, also signed as Lakes Road, and it soon skirts around the edge of a large fishing lake on the left. Pass the entrance to the lake and car park and follow the bridleway straight ahead, which winds under a huge viaduct of the railway that was crossed over earlier. The track then passes the isolated Floodgates Cottage and, shortly after, this look out for a track turning uphill on the left signed by a Peak and Northern footpath signpost (number 242) for Mellor and Cobden Edge.

3. Turn left up this path, which soon meets the railway again, and turn sharp right to cross it over a bridge. A distinct grass path, bearing slightly right, then leads to the edge of Mellor and Townscliffe golf course. The path has to negotiate a crossing of the golf course – so be wary of flying golfballs. From the edge of the golf course, walk uphill in the same general direction heading for a bench close to a cluster of trees. From the bench, keep going directly ahead under the trees and, when more fairways are reached, keep going in the same direction with woodland to your right. Golf balls may well pass you in the opposite direction (do not pick them up and chuck them in the trees, however tempted you may be). Halfway up the side of the woodland, keep a careful look out for a green waymarker signpost indicating paths for Cown Edge Way, Mellor and Gee Cross. Turn sharp left at this point and cross the fairways bearing slightly right towards woodland. Cross a little footbridge to join a hedge at the corner of the woodland on the far side of the woodland and a path leads to a track by the entrance to a scout camp.

4. Turn sharp right on the track signed for Mellor and Cobden Edge. This leads uphill on a tarmac drive, passing the golf clubhouse on the left before swinging left to join a lane. Follow the lane which turns sharp right in front of Tarden Farm riding stables and meanders around the hillside to reach a T-junction with another lane. Turn right here along Whetmorhurst Lane but, almost immediately,

leave it by joining the footpath on the left-hand side of the lane signed for Cobden Edge. The path is next to a driveway entrance and leads through two gate posts, over a stile by a gate, then bears left up and down a slope at the bottom of a large field. Turn right in the middle of the field and head directly uphill – the route is indicated by a waymarker on a telegraph pole. Head for the top left-hand corner of the field and cross a stile. Continue straight uphill alongside a wall but look back for breathtaking views across Greater Manchester and Cheshire. The walled path heads directly towards a house at the top of the hill and skirts around the side of the house, continuing up the driveway to reach a lane.

5. Turn right on the moorland lane which commands excellent views westward. Follow it for about 250 metres until a house is almost reached on the left close to a lane junction. Next to the house, take the path (indicated by a signpost on the left of the lane) which crosses a step-stile in the wall and heads uphill, bearing slightly right. Cross a derelict wall and reach a stile in the fence corner alongside a wall. Take a breather here and enjoy the best views to be had on this walk, with a panorama stretching from west to east, from the West Pennine Moors and the city centre to Kinder Scout. Closer at hand are Marple and the wooded Goyt Valley, Mellor church, Werneth Low and the Etherow Valley with Cown Edge and Longdendale to the north. The ridge you are standing on is marked on maps as Cobden Edge, but there are no great rock outcrops here – only rough pasture looking northward from the stile. Cross the stile and follow the wall-side to a step-stile in the next wall boundary. Continue across the middle of the next field, bearing slightly right and heading towards the county of Derbyshire – just a few fields away. On the far side of the field is another step-stile, cross this and go diagonally right across the corner of the next field to cross another step-stile and reach a wide track.

6. Turn right along this green track and head for the highest part of Mellor Moor. The triangulation pillar is passed in a field to the left. The track drops downhill to a crossroads of routes. Turn sharp left here along a signed footpath and pass the old quarry workings on the west face of Mellor Moor, in which stands a large cross erected by Marple Churches in 1970. On the opposite side of the valley stands Marple Ridge and, with good eyesight, you may be able to check on your car in the quarry car park. Walk up the tarmac drive past a

house called Three Chimneys and continue around the side of the hill on a grassy track between heather slopes and a wall. The track ends at a gate and stile; cross this and you are in the county of Derbyshire for the next few miles. The route leads across fields via a succession of stiles. Keep above the gorse slope before dropping down the hill to a stile in a fence line. Bear right diagonally across a field to another stile, then to another stile by a pond. Follow the fence alongside trees and the waymarked path leads uphill to a wall-side behind cottages and trees. At the waymarker signpost behind the trees turn sharp right, go downhill and cross a stile onto a drive by a pond. Follow the drive downhill to where it meets a lane.

7. Turn right and follow the lane to a crossroads by another golf course clubhouse. Turn right at the crossroads down a wide stone track signed for Shaw Farm. Keep to the track for the next half a mile and it gradually winds downhill to meet another lane. On the opposite side of the lane, there is a view of Whaley Moor, Park Moor and Cage Hill across the Goyt Valley. Turn right along the lane into the hidden hamlet of Brook Bottom. In front of the Fox Inn, look for signed paths leading off on either side of the lane and turn left down the wooded track signposted as the Goyt Way. Follow this pleasant track downhill for the next half a mile, it keeps above a steep-sided valley and eventually goes under the railway arch at Strines station (opened in 1866) in the valley bottom. Continue straight ahead along the cobbled road which becomes a lane and meanders over the River Goyt and past a textile mill (with a chimney that dominates the valley) and climbs uphill to meet the busy Marple-New Mills road at Strines village.

8. Take care and cross the road to join a track directly opposite signed as a private road. This track leads uphill and passes a row of cottages before reaching a tunnel beneath the high Peak Forest Canal. Do not go through the tunnel but turn right and climb the embankment to join the towpath. Turn right along this and follow the canal for the next half mile until the first stone bridge is reached. This is bridge number 21, crossed earlier in the walk. Leave the towpath and cross it again, but this time turn left on the far side of the bridge and follow the lane up past cottages with the canal down to your left. The lane climbs to a junction by the Romper Inn but do not pass the pub, instead turn right up the Ridge Road. Follow this for only 150 metres and the quarry car park is reached on the right.

20. Park Moor and Whaley Moor

This Cheshire walk begins along the Macclesfield Canal towpath then heads along the edge of Lyme Park to climb to the rock outcrops of Whaley Moor. It then heads south through undulating country on the edge of the Peak District before climbing up to the Gritstone Trail at Sponds Hill. It crosses Park Moor and descends through Lyme Park again with fantastic views across the Cheshire Plain. Most of the walk lies within the Peak District National Park.

Peaks and Panoramas: WHALEY MOOR has a distinctive ridge of rock outcrops and offers views towards Marple, Disley, New Mills and the Goyt Valley. SPONDS HILL, which has a triangulation pillar, is the highest point above PARK MOOR and the moorland slopes give extensive views particularly westwards across the Cheshire Plain and the southern half of the Manchester conurbation.

Distance: 11 miles

Map: Ordnance Survey Outdoor Leisure Sheet 1 The Peak District (Dark Peak Area)

Start: Nelson Pit Visitor Centre car park, off Anson Road, Higher Poynton, Cheshire (Grid Reference 945 833)

Getting there: From Poynton village centre go east out of the village for about a mile then take Anson Road which forks right and is signed for Middlewood Way parking (brown signpost). The road passes Anson Museum and reaches a T-junction close to the Boar's Head inn. Go straight across the T-junction and the free parking at Nelson Pit visitor centre is on your left between the Middlewood Way (disused railway line) and the Macclesfield Canal. The visitor centre is open daily.

Public transport: A bus service between Manchester and Middlewood, via Stockport, Hazel Grove and Poynton stops at the T-junction close to the Boar's Head Inn.

Background

It is, perhaps, surprising that Poynton has an industrial past lurking down its leafy lanes. Abandoned pits, mine shafts and disused railway inclines are the surviving legacy of a flourishing coal mining industry in Poynton which was linked to the dual transport corridors of the Macclesfield Canal and the Macclesfield, Bollington and Marple Railway. Lawrance Pit, the last working mine in the area, closed in 1935 and at Nelson Pit there is a new visitor centre and car park wedged between

The Macclesfield Canal at Higher Poynton

the canal and the former railway line. The Macclesfield Canal opened in 1831 and linked the Peak Forest Canal at Marple with the Trent and Mersey in the south. It was a major carrier of coal and Peak District limestone and provided a through route for traffic from Manchester to London.

The railway opened in 1869 and closed in 1970. After years of neglect, its recreational potential was finally realised and in 1985 it opened as the Middlewood Way, a countryside route for walkers, cyclists and horse riders. The tracks have, of course, been removed and even the old railway inclines which carried coal from Poynton mines to canal and railway have been opened up as rights of way.

From the moorland seat of Lyme Hall, the Legh family watched over the gradual development of Poynton, High Lane and Disley whilst pottering around their 1400 acre parkland estate. Lyme Park is an impressive National Trust property, at the heart of which lies the Elizabethan manor house. The deer park, granted in 1398, stretches through woodland up to Park Moor and the slopes of Sponds Hill. This walk skirts the boundary of National Trust land and offers fine views of the restored tower, the Cage, which sits squat upon Cage Hill. Lyme Park is often used for location filming when TV companies are churning out a period drama.

Park Moor and Whaley Moor are gritstone hills on the north-west edge of the Peak District which form an upland boundary between Derbyshire and Cheshire. The Peak District uplands ends here and to the west of Lyme Park lie the wooded pastures and ponds of the Cheshire Plain. It is nearly 30 miles to the west before any substantial hills start to rise again in Cheshire, when the sandstone escarpment of Helsby Hill is reached above Frodsham. But true uplands do not appear again until you hit the Clwydian Range in North Wales.

The Route

1. The car park at Nelson Pit is in two sections, walk through to the rear section which gives access onto the Macclesfield Canal alongside an information board. Turn left and follow the canal towpath in the opposite direction to the small marina. Follow the towpath for approximately three-quarters of a mile, passing a milestone (indicating Marple 3 miles to the north) and with views of the square Cage Hill tower upon the Lyme Park moorland rising to the east. When canal bridge number 13 is reached, go under it and leave the towpath on the left via a kissing gate. Turn left and cross the bridge to join a farm track. Follow the farm track for approximately 300 metres, passing cottages on the right, until a T-junction of tracks is reached at a stile and gate. Turn left here and follow the hedged track heading directly towards the Cage Hill tower until shortly a waymarked path is met crossing from the track from left to right.

2. Turn left here and cross the stile to follow a field-edge path down to another stile at the edge of woodland. Cross this stile and drop down through the wood to cross a footbridge, then up out of the other side of the wood to another stile. The path follows a field edge with the woodland immediately to your left. Keep to the field edge, crossing a step-stile in the boundary wall, until a cottage is reached on your right. There are good views to the left across a little valley to the village of High Lane. Go through the latch gate and pass the cottage on the right. Do not go through the white gate directly ahead, but look for the step-stile in the wall to the left, signed as Peak and Northern footpath number 119 to High Lane and Marple. Go over the stile and follow the wall-side down to cross a footbridge over a little brook. Immediately after this, cross the ladder stile over the wall onto National Trust land and also into the Peak District National Park. This path is kindly provided by the Trust – follow it up through the trees to meet the main driveway into Lyme Park and cross it, keeping the ticket booth to your right. Continue to the gates alongside the cottage called Red Lane Lodge. Go through the latch gate, locked at dusk.

3. Turn right along the footpath signed for Moorside, passing kennels on the left and following a reservoir access road. When the access road forks, take the left fork to leave the tarmac road and go uphill on an enclosed grass path signed a public footpath. Go over a stile and bear left, following the waymarked path around the farm buildings at Cockhead, overlooking Horse Coppice Reservoir. A signpost at a junction of paths is reached on the tarmac farm road just beyond the farm buildings. Take the path signed for Moorside which crosses a stile and keeps a fence and then a wall on the immediate right. The path runs along the north side of the Bollinhurst Reservoir. Keep the wall on your right and follow the path all the way around to the upper end of the reservoir, bearing right to reach a stile in the wall. Cross it and enter a wooded valley, crossing the brook, the reservoir inlet. Walk up the distinct path under the trees with the brook on the left. Cross a stile and enter a clearing with an enclosed wooded valley to the left. Continue straight uphill, bearing slightly right to reach a signpost at a junction of paths by a gate.

4. Do not go through the gate, instead turn sharp left along the path signposted for Green Lane. Do not follow the obvious track which leads around the back of the enclosed woodland but bear right off the track, keeping a derelict wall immediately to your right. Walk uphill to a stile, cross this and continue through the next field to another stile and onto a lane. Cross the stile almost opposite and follow the waymarked path through gorse to another stile at a field boundary. The rock outcrops along Whaley Moor can be seen to the right and the view opens out to the left towards Stockport and Manchester. Head diagonally right across the large field towards a wall corner and continue to the opposite side of the field where there is a gap in the wall next to a yellow-painted waymarker post. Go through the gap and turn right in the next field, keeping to the right of the telegraph wires to reach a footpath signpost standing in the middle of the field. Continue straight ahead to the wall gap next to an enclosed tree plantation. Turn right and follow the wall-side uphill to cross a waymarked ladder stile at the end of the Whaley Moor ridge. Follow

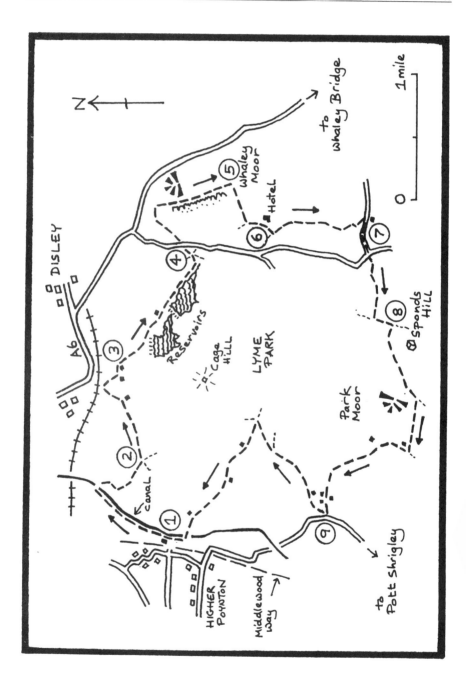

the ridge, heading southwards, for nearly half a mile. Keep the wall to the left and prominent rock outcrops to the right.

5. Whaley Moor ridge offers good views to the Kinder plateau in the east, Park Moor and Lyme Park to the south-west, but particularly northwards to the wooded Goyt Valley including Disley, the tall mill chimney at Strines and Marple. North of the Goyt can be seen Mellor Moor, Cown Edge and Werneth Low. Walk along the ridge until a wall is reached directly ahead – beyond this is the highest point of Whaley Moor, not accessible by right of way. Instead, turn sharp right near the wall and drop very steeply down from the ridge to a stile in a fence. Cross it and continue straight ahead, following a line which keeps to the right of the large hotel which can be seen below. There is a confusion of paths here, but cross a number of derelict walls, following a line just to the right of a small pond until a wooden waymarker signpost is reached by a cluster of trees. Turn left and follow the path which crosses a stile and heads directly to the nearby Moorside Hotel through rough pasture. Keep to the right of the hotel buildings, following the edge of the car park around to join the driveway entrance to the hotel.

6. Turn right to follow the driveway away from the hotel, but almost immediately look out for a stone track leading off from the drive where it sharply changes direction and heads for the nearby road. Join this track, crossing a cattle grid, and soon you swing left through a gateway and continue on a grassy track alongside a wall. The track is followed southwards for approximately three-quarters of a mile, forking right away from the wall and gradually dropping downhill to reach an abandoned farm next to a lane. Pass the farm buildings on the left and, on reaching the lane, turn sharp right and follow it downhill through woodland along a steep-sided valley. A brook is crossed and the lane then rises steeply to a road junction.

7. Take care and go straight across the junction to the stile and gate on the opposite side of the road. Cross the stile to join the path signposted for Lyme Park. The sunken path climbs uphill and swings left to an open gateway where there is an excellent view south-eastwards towards Kettleshulme. Go through a gateway and bear right, following the sunken path uphill with the wall to the right. Go through another gateway and continue in the same direction, heading directly uphill between two derelict walls. Eventually, the top of the ridge is reached next to a Peak and Northern footpath

sign and a wide green road is joined. Turn left and follow the old moorland road to cross a stile next to a gate. This route is part of the Gritstone Trail recreational path along the eastern moorland edge of Cheshire. The grassy track heading straight uphill leads to the summit of Sponds Hill, which has a triangulation pillar but little else.

8. The walk route, however, diverts right from the main track after the stile and follows the path signposted for Pott Shrigley. Turn right and head for a stile next to the wall on the right. Cross the stile and follow the grass track across the moor for the next half a mile, keeping the wall on the right. A stile and gate is reached, where the path forks. Leave the main track by taking the right fork and climb uphill to a nearby stile on the hillside. Cross the stile for excellent views westwards across the Cheshire Plain and north towards urban Stockport and Manchester. The path follows the wall-side downhill and goes through a gap in a wall at the bottom of the hill to join a track. Turn right and follow the track past a pretty cottage for approximately 100 metres to reach a stile in the wall on the left with a Peak and Northern signpost indicating a path to Higher Poynton. Cross the stile and follow the path diagonally across the field to cross a stream and continue downhill alongside a wall with a view right to Lyme Park. Keep the wall on the right and pass through two gates to join a stone access track to cottages. Follow this track downhill between cottages to reach a lane alongside a Methodist church.

9. Immediately turn right and follow the waymarked public footpath in front of the church. Follow this tarmac access road which bears right, crosses a stream and passes park lodges to reach a ladder stile where the track forks. Cross over the ladder stile and follow the grass track through a field for nearly half a mile to go through a kissing gate onto National Trust land. Follow the stone track, bearing slightly right for approximately 200 metres until another track joins from the right. Almost immediately, turn left and leave the main track, heading across rough and boggy pasture to reach a nearby ladder stile in a wall. Turn left and follow the stone track downhill to pass through the park gate next to the green-painted house. The path follows the farm track downhill for nearly three-quarters of a mile, passing a farm to eventually reach a bridge over the Macclesfield Canal next to a small marina. Cross over the road bridge and either follow the lane which swings right to reach the Nelson Pit visitor centre entrance on the right or rejoin the canal towpath and enter the rear of the car park on the left.

Appendix : The Hills Explored

The following is a list of over 50 hills, moors and landmarks explored in this book arranged in order of height above sea level in metres. The list starts with Marple Ridge, the lowest, and ends with Hoarstone Edge, the highest. Each is numbered and can be found on the adjoining location plan for easy reference. Some summits (e.g. Higher Hill) have not been reached on the walks but the height given is for the highest point. Also, in some cases (e.g. Longworth Moor, Rooley Moor) where a moorland has no discernible summit, the height has been estimated from the Ordnance Survey map.

To convert metres to feet, multiply by 3.2808. Or, close enough – and much simpler – multiply by 3 and add 10 percent.

Feature	Ht/m	Feature	Ht/m
1. Marple Ridge	209	27. Rooley Moor	400
2. Werneth Low War Memorial	240	28. Brown Wardle Hill	400
3. Affetside	270	29. Middle Hill	400
4. Idle Hill (Werneth Low ridge)	279	30. Crook Hill	408
5. Hartshead Pike	280	31. Whaley Moor	410
6. Cobden Edge	310	32. Park Moor (Sponds Hill)	410
7. Mellor Moor	327	33. Windy Hill	416
8. Cheetham Close	329	34. Bull Hill	418
9. Longworth Moor	335	35. Knowl Hill	419
10. Peel Tower	340	36. Pots and Pans	427
11. Turton Heights	343	37. Hades Hill	433
12. Wharmton Hill	348	38. Rough Hill	434
13. Harrop Edge	348	39. Alderman Hill	440
14. Ox Hey Top	360	40. Millstone Edge	448
15. Rivington Pike	362	41. Rape Hill	450
16. Harcles Hill	371	42. Slades Rocks	450
17. Bishop Park Monument	375	43. Dick Hill	453
18. Broadhead Noddle	376	44. Green Hole Hill	453
19. Badger Edge	379	45. Higher Hill	456
20. Crompton Moor	391	46. Winter Hill	456
21. Turton Moor	394	47. White Hill	466
22. Harridge Pike	395	48. Scout Moor (Whittle Pike)	467
23. Top of Pike	398	49. Blackstone Edge	472
24. Tame Scout	398	50. Top of Leach (inc Hailstorm Hill)	474
25. Hollingworthall Moor	399	51. Hoarstone Edge	497
26. Cown Edge/Coombes Rocks	400		

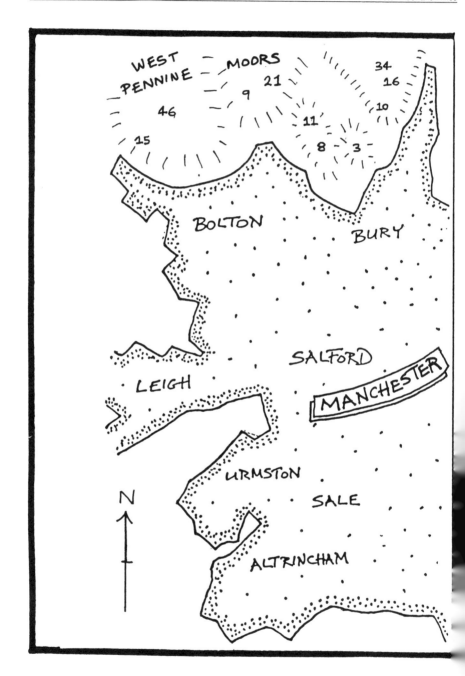

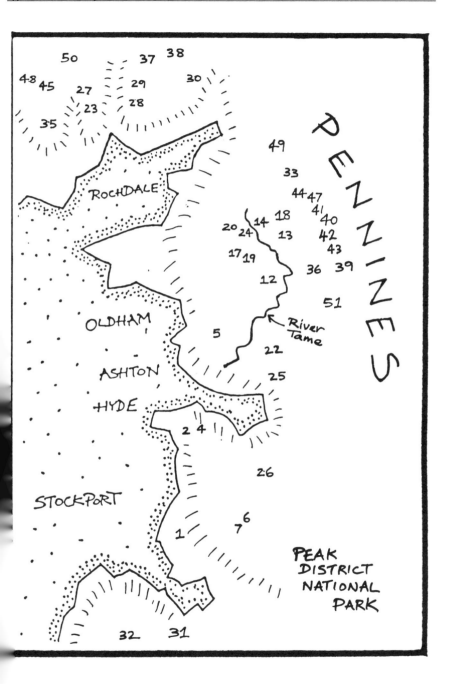

ALSO OF INTEREST:

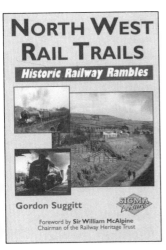

NORTH WEST RAIL TRAILS
Gordon Suggitt

Discover the North West by walking the region's former railways! These 25, mostly circular routes from 2 to 5 miles give an insight into how the the railways influenced the industries, towns and countryside of Lancashire and Greater Manchester. Many of the walks contain sections of canal paths and pass through landscape as varied as tramroads, country park, and nature reserve. Easy-to-follow descriptions are accompanied by clear sketch maps and photographs of classic trains and locos. £6.95

RAMBLES AROUND MANCHESTER
Mike Cresswellphotographs, Reg Timms

Take the bus or train from the city centre and discover the treats around Manchester. "Written with fun, rare talent and impish humour" BOLTON EVENING NEWS.£ 6.95

THE THIRLMERE WAY: a long-distance walk from Manchester to the Lake District
Tim Cappelli

Mancunians interested in the origins of their water supply and all those who enjoy an unusual series of walks will enjoy this guidebook - "Well-researched; written by a very responsible and diligent author" THE WESTMORLAND GAZETTE. £6.95

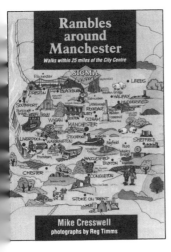

GREATER MANCHESTER WALKS WITH CHILDREN
Nick Lambert

Each walk in this ' Walks with Children' title has been carefully planned with kids in mind. Directions are clear and concise, and feature a handy 'escape route' to cut the walk short. A narrative written 'just for them' is included

Greater Manchester
WALKS with CHILDREN

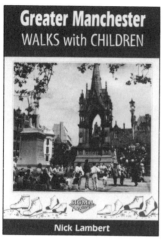

Nick Lambert

FIFTY CLASSIC
WALKS IN LANCASHIRE

SIGMA
TERRY MARSH

alongside the route instructions, guiding them along the route, pointing out the sights, wildlife and history. Questions and quizzes are also featured to engage their minds and imaginations. £6.95

DISCOVERY WALKS IN LANCASHIRE
Brian Conduit

This guide contains 30 routes of varying lengths and terrain. All walks have a heritage theme and enable you to appreciate both Lancashire's rich historical legacy as well as its ever-changing landscape. They take in Roman remains, medieval castles and abbeys, nature reserves, country parks and (of course) the many monuments to the country's role in the industrial revolution. "An impressive variety of walks...rounded off with some fascinating details on interesting features" BLACKPOOL GAZETTE. £6.95

50 CLASSIC WALKS IN LANCASHIRE
Terry Marsh

"The walking country of Lancashire ranks amongst the finest in the British Isles" says Terry Marsh, author. Terry writes with the determined aim of enlightening those whose image of the county is unfavourable. He reveals Lancashire at its diverse best - from wild woodland expanses and witch country, to tranquil river valleys. £7.95

All of our books are available from your local bookshop. In case of difficulty, or to obtain our complete catalogue, please contact:

Sigma Leisure, 1 South Oak Lane, Wilmslow,
Cheshire SK9 6AR
Phone: 01625-531035
Fax: 01625-536800
E-mail: info@sigmapress.co.uk
http://www.sigmapress.co.uk
MASTERCARD and VISA orders welcome.